JOURNEYS IN SERVICE

Gaurav Madan

N
NOT TO SCALE

JAMMU & KASHMIR

HIMACHAL
PRADESH

PUNJAB

UTTARANCHAL

HARYANA

DELHI

ARUNACHAL
PRADESH

RAJASTHAN

UTTAR
PRADESH

SIKKIM

ASSAM   NAGALAND

BIHAR

MEGHALAYA

MANIPUR

MADHYA PRADESH

JHARKHAND

TRIPURA

MIZORAM

AHMEDABAD

I N D I A

WEST BENGAL

GUJARAT

CHHATTISGARH

MAHARASHTRA

ORISSA

ARABIAN SEA

ANDRA PRADESH

BAY OF BENGAL

GOA

KARNATAKA

LAKSHADWEEP

TAMIL NADU

ANDAMAN AND NICOBAR ISLANDS
(INDIA)

KERALA

INDIAN OCEAN

● | Indicorps Fellowship project sites

The international boundaries on this map are neither claimed to be correct nor authenticated by the Survey of India directives.

CONTENTS

I DOUBLE DARE YOU

by Pavi Krishnan

the edges of things are
always deceptive.

because we are taught to
believe in endings and
beginnings.

but the truth is:

There Are No Borders.

and all boundaries are lines
drawn in the imagination
(like the equator)

people like to put things
in their places.

(we believe in belonging
somewhere)

this is the problem with poetry

(it does not understand belonging)

and it will not be put in place.

with crayons on paper maybe

but who can live life strictly

inside-the-lines?

the color of countries that

cannot be contained

in cliches where

the red of your heart spills

into the red of the rose spills

into the red of the sunset spills

into mehendi on the hands of a bride.

and who can explain these things?

but what i want to know is simple:

who settled the sky on top of
the mountain

and who drew the restless
margins of the sea?

everything flows into everything else.

like a picture drawn without once

lifting pencil from paper;

this world.

now tell me the story of your life

(whoever you are) go on

i Double Dare you!

tell me the story of your life

without once touching mine.

FOREWORD

by Senator Harris Wofford

In this short and inspiring book, the story of the founding of Indicorps and the stories of the experience of some of the first Indicorps Fellows come alive. They add a new chapter to the long history of the criss-crossing of the globe between America and India — between the land that became the modern world's first democracy and the subcontinent that contained one of the world's oldest societies that is now the most populous democracy. Those journeys have involved the movement of ideas as well as people, and the Indicorps experience involves both, in a unique new form.

As one who undertook one of those journeys long ago, in 1949, as a twenty-three year old, just out of college, with a one-year fellowship to India to study Mahatma Gandhi, I read this book with a very sympathetic eye. It will stir many diverse readers, as it has stirred me, to recount and remember their passages to India, and compare their experiences with those of these Indicorps Fellows. But above all I hope it is a book that will be read by many young professionals of the Indian diaspora — in the United States, United Kingdom, Canada, Australia, Hong Kong and elsewhere. And I hope many will be tempted to undertake their own great adventure before the pressures of career and family put that out of reach.

Ten times I've been to India since an unforgettable month as a boy of twelve in 1938 when I went there with my grandmother on a low-cost travel program called Tramp Trips. We were going around the world in 180 days. India was the longest and most exciting part of our six-month globe-circling on the eve of World War II.

Three times in the 1960s I went to India on behalf of President Kennedy's Peace Corps, which in its early years sent more than a thousand Volunteers to serve there for two years. In 1977, my wife and

I went back in the aftermath of the world's largest free election, when power peacefully passed from Indira Gandhi's Congress Party to the opposition.

It is from still vivid experience in India that I appreciate what an opportunity and challenge Indicorps presents to each Indicorps Fellow. That's why the stories in this book delight me and make me want Indicorps to continue to grow. The Fellows have much to offer the India of their heritage and, on their return, much to offer their current homelands.

As an American, I've long been struck by how far back our ties to India go, and how great our need is now for a better understanding of India and the whole developing world. After all, Columbus encountered America while on a journey to find a short-cut to the legendary riches of India. Five years before the Mayflower sailed to America, the British East India Company set foot in India.

Fast forward to the 20th century struggle for Indian independence during which the ideas of the American Revolution in the Declaration of Independence were often invoked by Jawaharlal Nehru, who became India's first Prime Minister. Mahatma Gandhi drew on Thoreau's essay on Civil Disobedience in making his case for a strategy of non-violent direct action, and adopted Thoreau's term as the name for the jail-going he preached and practiced. So the criss-crossing between India and America, which Indicorps is continuing, has resulted in a remarkable reciprocal trade of ideas.

For Clare and me, our fellowship was a powerful experience of cross-cultural education. India was an unparalleled school for world citizenship. I am sure it remains a School of the World for Indicorps Fellows — for leadership in our complex, interdependent world.

In the India of 1949, for me the biggest question to pursue was Gandhi and his message, but in the decade of Martin Luther King, Gandhi's message seemed to have migrated to America, and thence to South Africa with Nelson Mandela. For most Indicorps Fellows, as the stories in this book indicate, other more pressing questions will take priority. In dealing with almost any great pending problem in the world, India has experience that is relevant.

Nowhere on earth is there more pluralism than in India, with ancient kinds of discrimination built into the culture, not just between Hindus and Muslims, Sikhs and Buddhists, but within Hinduism itself, with the age-old caste structure waning yet still powerful. And nowhere is there greater need to make One out of Many, exemplified by the rise of the Dalits, whose caste once made them "untouchable" but whom Gandhi called *Harijans* — "children of God" (now also an unacceptable designation).

Our fellowship in India shaped my later life. Time and again with Gandhi's followers around India I was asked what I had done to end racial segregation in America, or, more sharply, whether I had gone to jail in protest. Usually I resisted the temptation to taunt Indians about their deeply-ingrained caste discrimination, but the challenge did sting. I had done nothing about what, from India, seemed so clearly to be the heaviest burden on the American soul.

Upon returning to America, in the book *India Afire* which Clare and I wrote together, and in other writings and talks, I tried to distill Gandhi's current relevance to our civil rights struggle, and urged the civil rights movement to adopt an American version of a Gandhian strategy. I enrolled in Howard University Law School and became the first white man to graduate. A widely circulated convocation talk I gave at Hampton Institute in 1955 (a few weeks before the Montgomery bus boycott) provoked letters from civil rights leaders who said Gandhi's strategy would never work in America. One dean of Howard University who had talked and walked with Gandhi wrote me that he had sadly concluded that there was no Gandhi possible among

American blacks. That was just a few weeks before the Montgomery bus boycott began.

Dr. Martin Luther King rose to national leadership, and to the Nobel Peace Prize, because Rosa Parks went to jail. The previous summer, she had attended a workshop on Gandhi and non-violent action, and told herself that some day she just might have the courage for civil disobedience. That day came during the Christmas holiday season in 1955 when she refused to move to the back of the bus for a white man. In response, the boycott was launched, led by the 26-year old pastor who had immersed himself in Gandhi's writings a few years earlier.

Large-scale non-violent action followed: student sit-ins, Freedom Rides, jail-going, and the politics of marching, climaxed by the vast March on Washington in 1963 and the four-day march from Selma to Montgomery in 1965. Together black and white Americans, often invoking Gandhi's name and words, with the leadership of President Johnson and the Congress, two far-reaching civil rights acts were enacted by Congress, and at long last ended public racial segregation and won the right to vote for all American citizens.

Thanks to my Indian experience and writing on Gandhi, King welcomed me as a volunteer strategist and enlisted me to help write the section on his road to non-violence in his first book, *Stride Toward Freedom*. When I suggested that he go to India and meet with Nehru and some of the still-living colleagues of Gandhi, he readily said yes, and we secured funds to help him do so. With his wife Coretta he went for two weeks in 1959, calling it his "pilgrimage."

So it was a sentimental journey, a few weeks after the Inauguration of Barack Obama, to go on a Congressional delegation led by civil rights hero and current Representative John Lewis to help commemorate the 50th anniversary of King's trip. We went on King's trail, starting in New Delhi with the opening of an extraordinary exhibit linking Gandhi, King, and Obama. At the entrance was a huge photograph of Obama in his Senate office, pointing to the pictures he had on the wall behind his desk. Obama said they gave him inspiration every day: Gandhi at his spinning wheel, King giving his "I Have a Dream" speech at the Lincoln Memorial, the Selma to Montgomery marchers, President Kennedy with King and Civil Rights leaders in the Oval Office, and Abraham Lincoln.

The high point of that most recent trip to India was a meeting at Gandhi's former ashram in Ahmedabad with a group of Indicorps Fellows and Indicorps co-founder Roopal Shah. Talking with them, listening to their stories and questions, took me back sixty years to the time when Clare and I set forth on our fellowship with much the same spirit shown by those Indicorps Fellows. We did not render the service of an Indicorps Fellow or a Peace Corps Volunteer but we went up, and down India, probing the past and present of Indian politics, including Gandhi's historic successes and India's tragic failures — the riots and partition.

When we came home a few months early with cases of amoebic dysentery, the cure then was months of weekly shots of arsenic in our butts. "Arsenic is an amazing medicine," our doctor said. "One ounce will cure; ten ounces would kill." Clare, who never shared my enthusiasm for Gandhi, commented: "That's what I think about civil disobedience."

Each class of Indicorps Fellows no doubt will have their own differences of view, and group tensions to overcome. Aspects of life in India may be hard but the effective early Peace Corps recruiting poster should be recalled: "The hardest job you'll ever love." Real education does not come easily, and is often what you look back on and realize later as you remember.

On my fourth visit in India, in 1961, assisting Peace Corps Director Sargent Shriver, Prime Minister Nehru agreed to welcome Peace Corps Volunteers to India, initially to the Punjab where the provincial government requested them. He went on to urge Shriver to warn the

Senator Harris Wofford visited Indicorps-Ahmedabad at the Gandhi Ashram in February 2009. Wofford's interactions fascinated the team. He explained how both Gandhi and King valued the power of the struggle.

young Americans that for hundreds or thousands of years outsiders had swept onto the plains of the Punjab, and then finally they left or were absorbed, but the Punjab remained much the same. He didn't want them to be disappointed when for all their effort the Punjab remained much as it was.

However difficult it may be to measure the long-term effect that the work of Indicorps Fellows or Peace Corps Volunteers may have on India or the effect their experience in India will have on them, I've seen how the Punjab has changed after partition and the green revolution. And I know how experience in India can affect one's life.

Also pertinent to Indicorps is the less known side of Gandhi's double-edged sword of non-violent action that King often emphasized: civil disobedience was one cutting edge when necessary, but one's other duty was for constructive service. Gandhi called on the Indian National Congress to require its members to participate regularly in a program of service and social invention that included action to end the ancient Hindu caste system's discrimination, to teach illiterate Indians to read and write, to create small village industries, and to assure public sanitation in every community.

In line with this, King wanted the Southern Christian Leadership Conference he headed to act in the same spirit. When angry young blacks raised the banner of "Black Power" and some called for violence, or joined in riots that burned parts of many cities, King said the right watchwords were not "Burn baby burn!" but "Build baby build!" and "Learn baby learn!"

This excursion in history is the background in which I read *Journeys in Service*, and salute Indicorps, the social invention and dedicated work of Roopal, Sonal and Anand Shah. I don't predict necessarily that a young Gandhi or Martin Luther King or Rosa Parks will emerge, shaped by the experience as an Indicorps Fellow, but I do expect unpredictable, important and creative outcomes.

Gandhi named his autobiography, *Story of My Experiments with Truth*. Each Fellow will have a story, as the moving stories in this new book so well demonstrate. There are many new chapters of this story to be written by the Fellows to come. And each story will be a modern-day Experiment with Truth.

Senator Harris Wofford

"If you have come to help me, you are wasting your time. But if you have come because your liberation is bound up with mine, then let us work together."

— Lila Watson

A NEW RITE OF PASSAGE

by Roopal Shah and Anand Shah

The Indicorps story began at an inflection point in India's journey. Fifty years after independence and ten years into a slightly liberalized economy, India was just beginning to show signs of confidence on the international stage. The Indian diaspora continued to grow in the United States, and from all measures were among the most successful immigrant groups. The Indian establishment saw the outflow of people as a brain drain. People from all walks of life lined up outside embassies for decade-long procedures for emigration opportunities to the United States or Britain. Top talent left India searching for opportunities to reach their potential, and saw India as a country frozen in time.

Yet, those born and/or raised outside of India longed for a relationship with India that would complete an unconscious quest to understand their cross-cultural identities. Empowered with the idealism and values that enabled the rapid rise of the immigrant community, Indians abroad that were coming of age also saw a rising India as unprecedented opportunity to make a difference in a country that was distant, yet peculiar in its familiarity.

The creative tension between those wanting to leave India and the progeny of those who left suggested unprecedented potential to mobilize an increasingly sophisticated diaspora with a common denominator: India. An emerging generation of idealistic and hard-working young people of Indian origin, longing to contribute to and understand their homeland, could just be the catalyst that turned a brain drain into a "brain gain" that applied their talent and global exposure to the frontlines of India's development.

Indicorps was conceived as an experiment to legitimize a year of service to India as a rite of passage. The product would be young leaders with impeccable values: refined by the deep history of Indian service movements, weathered by the hard reality of grassroots efforts for change, and permanently motivated by the power of individual action. In theory, Indicorps was plausible. Making it happen was the challenge.

The application process for Indicorps' inaugural year represented the stark generational conflicts in the Indian immigrant diaspora. A prospective Fellow avoided telling his mother about his interest in the program until he decided to matriculate. His mother called the Indicorps office; though complimentary of the idea of Indicorps for her retirement, she was livid about how the program would derail her son's medical career. Another parent, steeped in India's spiritual teachings, sought a virtual guarantee of his daughter's safety in the country he called home. Yet another, while on a trip to India, refused to visit her daughter 250 kilometers away in a village, saying "I left India for a reason." The irony was absurd: applicants embodied their parents' passion for and connection to India, but faced the latter's irrational fear that serving in India would undermine the immigrant dream. A bystander once joked that everyone admires Gandhi, but no one wants their child to be Gandhi.

The challenge was in our face: making Indicorps work meant causing an attitude shift. We had to make the idea of serving in India noble and prestigious. Few imagined that second- and third-generation Indians would willingly give back to the country of their heritage. To convince parents, students and young adults, we hit the road. We spoke everywhere — in Marathi Mandals, Telugu societies, Oriya conventions; at art exhibits, dance performances, others' fundraisers, temples, mosques, gurudwaras, cultural events; on college campuses, with Indian professional associations, outside bhangra blowouts, during the SABA Hawaiian Happy Hour, at a dinner gathering at someone's house — wherever someone would let us talk about the value of service and India.

The idea was provocative. To some, it was contagious. Many young Indian-Americans jumped out of their seats to help publicize, write, volunteer, take pictures, whatever they could do. Several even came to India to help. Others told us we were crazy. Some said it would be impossible to do. The power of Indicorps' attraction was in its simplicity: if you are considering service in some other part of the world, why not consider starting with your own country of origin? A young Indian-American politician attending a discussion in Chicago captured it best, saying "I would have thought this already existed."

In America, Indicorps fielded criticism from Indians for bringing people of Indian origin back to India; in India, it was precisely that Indians were willing to come back to India that made the idea so powerful. The response in India was a combination of admiration and disbelief. The predominant way of giving for Indians abroad had always been donations and remittances. Our message involved no money at all. Indicorps was about giving time and skills, because a first-hand relationship with the issues of India seemed the most compelling way to unlock priceless resources. Even money follows people. The message of service — young people acting on their belief in India's potential — resonated with grassroots community-based organizations, government officials, corporate leaders, and local communities.

Our philosophy was simple: help organizations working strenuously on the ground to find the kind of people they need to do things they wish they could do. We reached out to grassroots-level organizations throughout India to help them structure hands-on projects appropriately to attract talent, with one caveat: projects should require Indicorps' Fellows to immerse in the community. In return, we promised these organizations that we would nurture a genre of volunteers that were committed, intense, and willing to do whatever was necessary to succeed.

In the early years, many grassroots organizations thought Indicorps required too much effort on their part to get a Fellow, especially because the Fellows did not come with monetary contributions. Today, several organizations have waited patiently for years for the opportunity to engage an Indicorps Fellow.

To honor our promise to organizations, Indicorps invests heavily in reducing the burden that an unprepared volunteer would have on a grassroots organization's resources: We conduct an intensive month-long orientation. We track each Fellow's progress throughout the year and buttress their personal motivation on weekly phone calls. We organize quarterly workshops to provide ongoing training and a space to share learnings, to reflect with peers, and to recalibrate commitment.

The Indicorps Orientation is by far the most intense month any of these Fellows have ever experienced: We provide basic training in everything from gendered interactions, language, and experiential community people skills. We cultivate empathy and understanding. We promote self-reliance, self-discovery, and humility. But mostly we dismantle fear to enable positive constructive steps towards change.

To Fellows, we promise an unparalleled opportunity to nurture transformative leadership capacity. At Indicorps, change is about being an exemplar: true leadership is a product of values and character. Mahatma Gandhi articulated this idea when he said "my life is my message." How they serve is as important as choosing to serve, and who our Fellows become is as important as what they do on the ground. We gave our service leadership theory a motto: Service for the Soul.

Indicorps takes a personal interest in the success of each and every Fellow. Projects rarely go as expected; each Fellow is individually mentored and encouraged to learn as much from what does not work as from what does. Many Fellows have succeeded wildly — Fellows have been pivotal in developing local women's health insurance schemes, sports leadership programs, rural design schools, rural water solutions, community radio programs, employability initiatives, etc. However, the true power is in what the group represents over time. The impact is captured by a prospective Fellow after an Indicorps alumni gathering: "I had never met such a fearless group — many 20-somethings who had deferred law school or government jobs to throw their stuff in a backpack and live in pretty much under any conditions for the chance to make a difference."

A decade into the Indicorps experiment, we have witnessed an explosion of opportunities from within India and around the globe. Indicorps constantly promoted the power of youth-led public service programs, and even assisted in the launch of other programs providing opportunities for Indians serving India such as Connect India, Piramal Fellowship, Teach for India, Inspire Now, the Gandhi Fellowship, MedicIndia, Learning Journey, etc. Numerous Indicorps partner organizations, now more optimistic about the value of dedicated individuals, have also created structured volunteer opportunities of their own.

Margaret Mead once said: "Never doubt that a small group of thoughtful, committed citizens can change the world. Indeed, it is the only thing that ever has." We have been asked to scale our success and increase the number of Fellows exponentially. Instead, we continue to search for the handful of dedicated people who are insatiably obsessed with making the world a better place, and give them the tools to realize their potential. Who they become, and what they do, will define Indicorps' success for years to come.

Roopal Shah and Anand Shah

Beyond Relief

In 2001, a devastating earthquake rocked the state of Gujarat, epi-centering in the rural district of Kutch. Gandhi Ashram-based Manav Sadhna was one of many local organizations who responded to the crisis; they took a distinctive participatory approach to disaster relief. For three subsequent years, six Indicorps Fellows and Manav Sadhna extended efforts beyond relief and rehabilitation, strengthening craft, nurturing creative identity, sustaining women's livelihoods, and providing clean drinking water. Their collective efforts re-defined the meaning of community-building.

On January 26, 2001, a massive earthquake struck Kutch, leaving over 20,000 dead and a wake of damage and destruction. Relief efforts began almost immediately, with a flood of government and release workers arriving to help rebuild the towns and villages that had crumbled in the disaster. A barren landscape, Kutch is marked by a harsh climate, severe lack of water, and significant isolation. The aesthetic is inescapable. The traditional *bhungas* (round mud huts) are scattered amongst the hardened, cracked earth. The blinding sun and arid land are juxtaposed with the vibrancy and color of life.

Here from the edge of India, is an account of the multi-faceted partnership between the women and men of rural Kutch, Gandhi Ashram-based non-profit organization Manav Sadhna, and six Indicorps Fellows who over three years journeyed far from what they knew to discover a new idea of community. In 2002, Shezeen Suleman and Radhika Singh arrived in Kutch as part of the inaugural Indicorps Fellowship class. In 2003, Samina Akbari and Anjali Desai focused on creativity and artisanship. And in 2004, Rishi Kotiya and Rupal Soni concentrated on financial independence and community ownership.

It is a story characterized by Indicorps' and Manav Sadhna's unique commitment to fully investing in communities, where each act represents larger purpose. Nearly a decade later, we can see the lasting strength of these relationships, the value of unrivaled perseverance, and the impact made by those who were able to see beyond disaster and relief. But to understand the story fully, we must go back even further.

An Inclusive Response

In February 2001, a year and a half prior to the arrival of the first Indicorps Fellows, Manav Sadhna adopted Ludiya, a cluster of village hamlets approximately 30 kilometers from the Indo-Pakistan border. At the time, Ludiya's residents were on the verge of a mass migration. Manav Sadhna sought to approach the situation on the ground as a people's program, operating in the Gandhian tradition of *swaraj* (self-reliant governance), with participation and input on both relief and rehabilitation driven by the community. "We felt that nothing [sustainable] would happen by giving things for free. There were lots of people giving things for free, but there were few willing to join hands and work with people themselves," says Jayesh *bhai* Patel, co-founder of Manav Sadhna.

While most organizations focused heavily on building homes, Manav Sadhna started by building relationships. This began with organizing public morning and evening prayers through Koran readings with a *maulvi* (Islamic teacher), providing health services, and constructing four *anganwadis* (pre-schools). From the very initial phases the organization cooperated with the community to address the great need for health care, decent education, and access to drinking water.

Ludiya, encompassing the new hamlet of Gandhi Nu Gaam, was the first village to be rebuilt even though many other villages had far more in the way of physical supplies and even volunteer manpower.

Manav Sadhna & Gramshree
www.manavsadhna.org
www.gramshree.org

Based in the Sabarmati Gandhi Ashram (Gujarat), Manav Sadhna's guiding philosophy is to "Love All, Serve All". Officially registered in 1995, Manav Sadhna engages in constructive humanitarian projects that cut across barriers of class and religion. Manav Sadhna focuses on values-based education, community building, health/sanitation, nutrition, and women's empowerment. In 2001, after the devastating earthquake in Gujarat, Manav Sadhna shifted its base to Ludiya, Kutch and devoted nine months on relief and rehabilitation efforts. Sister organization Gramshree sustains livelihoods for women and serves as a catalyst towards financial independence, self-reliance, and awareness.

Beyond Relief

COLLABORATE Rupal Soni and Rishi Kotiya speak to women in Gandhi Nu Gaam about setting a price for their embroidery. In 2004-05, these fellows helped create an "otlo" or fixed price marketplace that gave all of the artisans a platform to show and sell their craft.

DELIBERATE In 2002, Shezeen Suleman inspects the wall of a local dam with Jayeshbhai and engineers from a nearby watershed management group.

Manav Sadhna relocated to ground zero of the response efforts in Ludiya to address basic humanitarian needs — drinking water, health services, and immediate shelter. Within the year, Manav Sadhna seamlessly shifted from response to recovery, actively rebuilding alongside villagers through local, participatory measures. Indicorps' projects then followed over the subsequent three years, furthering the commitment to these communities, beyond recovery and disaster relief.

A Continuing Investment

In 2002, at the age of 21, Shezeen Suleman arrived in Ludiya with an educational background in watershed management and international development from the University of Toronto. Shezeen is of Kutchi ancestry and was the first in four generations to return to India. Shezeen's project was to help ensure the availability of safe and adequate drinking water in Ludiya and surrounding villages. "I brought my thousand page hydrology book from college thinking it would be the best resource I had, and it was utterly useless. I had to re-learn how to learn," she remembers.

Starting with what she describes as "a thousand cups of *chai*" with people across the area, Shezeen learned the value of the knowledge that does not always appear in textbooks or Western universities. What was particularly fascinating was the ability of the local people to identify areas where fresh water would be found without any geological surveys or equipment. Over the year, Shezeen partnered with a diverse array of local leaders, masons, and laborers, building check dams and wells in search of an effective system to provide an adequate supply of water. Today, these wells still provide water in the parched climate.

At the same time and also with the backing of Indicorps and Manav Sadhna, Radhika Singh initiated the Rural Design School to facilitate the development of women's skill, creativity, and expression, as well as incorporate embroidery into a livelihood. From the very beginning the project faced a number of challenges. Partly due to tourism, and partly due to post-earthquake relief, a certain "relief mentality" was created. Through an excess supply of unnecessary items, a culture of dependency and entitlement developed and persisted. "The relief efforts undermined the local culture. An attitude was created where people were constantly asking for things. Supplies were distributed irresponsibly and to date the culture has not recovered from this destruction," describes Anar *behn* Patel, co-founder of Manav Sadhna and Gramshree, a women's empowerment organization.

From the start, overcoming this mentality was one of the many hurdles that the Indicorps project faced. For the Rural Design School, one core question became, "How do you preserve integrity, pride, and creativity in embroidery?" Samina Akbari and Anjali Desai grappled with this question as they carried forward the Rural Design School project in 2003-2004.

Walking from village to village, Samina and Anjali ran a school out of their backpacks, calling meetings amongst the brightly-painted *bhungas*, and organizing women to think differently about not only their craft, but also about their potential. Samina and Anjali often walked for kilometers at a stretch between villages in the unforgiving mid-day heat. Their endeavors required persistence and great patience, as they went house to house to gather women and conduct classes over the din of babies, goats, and the hullaballoo of women asking for payment.

The first step was having the women stop thinking of their embroidery only as a means to make money, but also as a way of self-expression and identity. The Fellows created a full curriculum with weekly lesson plans, and provided a regular space for women to interact with one another. While there was always constant commotion, women consistently attended classes even after money was removed from the equation. The weekly classes became an open space for interaction between women. More impressively, the mobile Rural Design School became a safe space the women could claim as their own.

The classes Samina and Anjali taught began with small affirmations of confidence and creativity. In a place where most women could not read or write, having women pick up a pencil to draw their own designs was a task in itself. Thus, one of the first activities was simply drawing a tree. Samina shares, "Just picking up the pencil was intimidating. It was something completely foreign." From this initial drawing, women discussed their portrayals explaining their individual perspectives. Eventually they embroidered over the preliminary drawings. This activity was instrumental in showing the women that they were capable of venturing outside of what they already knew, and equally capable of coming up with their own designs.

Today women do not even hesitate. They are equally comfortable designing, producing and marketing products on their own, as they are with embroidering under Gramshree's oversight and quality control. Additionally, women have begun to incorporate the designs that come from Gramshree into their own personal works, interpreting and innovating single-handedly. "If we continue learning, we can go far. My thinking now is I want to go to Delhi, Bombay, and see new places," says Mana *behn* Seva, arguably Gandhi Nu Gaam's most prolific and confident artisan.

Borrowing from the time-honored Muslim and *Harijan* (Dalit) embroidery traditions, Samina and Anjali collaborated with women to improve their skills, while consistently emphasizing the women's own creative expression and abilities. From eliciting original designs to taking women on exposure trips to other villages and towns where embroidery work was done, Samina and Anjali saw innovation and creativity become a part of the pride the women had in their handicrafts and heritage. Most women had never left their villages, not even for childbirth. So in 2005 when Rishi Kotiya and Rupal Soni — the next

LOOK, LISTEN, LEARN *Anjali Desai discusses ideas about designs with women in Ludiya. By building on the strengths of the community, the Indicorps team developed meaningful relationships that were instrumental in the progress of the Rural Design School project after the 2001 earthquake.*

CREATE *Traditional embroidery remains a strong part of the identity, livelihoods, and pride of women in Kutch.*

Fellows to continue the Rural Design School — organized a trip to Ahmedabad, the excitement was palpable. The women displayed their handicrafts in the big city and were thrilled with the positive response. "There is a visible change in the confidence women have in themselves, and this is a reflection of the village's growth and development," remarks Anjali, who has stayed on in India since 2003, and continues her engagement with the women of Ludiya and Gramshree.

In 2004, Rishi and Rupal continued forward with the vision of a fair and inclusive marketplace. Alongside the residents of Gandhi Nu Gaam, they organized the construction of an *otlo*, a thatch-covered open veranda where each artisan could sell her embroidered goods. The objective was to create a fair, fixed-price marketplace from where busloads of tourists could experience and support authentic artisanship. The *otlo* also enabled a sense of transparency, where each product could be displayed, and each sale celebrated as a community benefit.

Not Without Hardship

Indicorps' three-year journey in Kutch was not always smooth. One of the biggest challenges was balancing the need for financial earning with creating a belief amongst women that there was inherent value in their own design and creativity. Fellows endured countless pleas and lengthy discussions about payment. They surmounted internal tensions between individuals and families within the village. They also faced a host of personal challenges that come with leaving one's comfort zone, trying to enable change in a place steeped in tradition, and tirelessly pushing themselves in such a harsh environment. Samina reflects, "I was burnt to a crisp. I lost fifty pounds. I had diarrhea for the whole year. I was robbed... and it was one of the best years of my life. I loved it."

Today there still remain a host of challenges. In the neighboring village of Ashashpura, villagers complain that they are not formally recognized by the government and therefore do not have access to government benefits and services. The *sarpanch* (head of village council) of Ludiya, Veeyal Alim Node, says the people of his village still do not put enough emphasis on their children's education. Agriculture continues to remain heavily dependent on the rains, and while water is available, it is in no way abundant. Despite these challenges, strides have been made. Initially, for example, many men were skeptical of their wives' involvement with the Rural Design School project. Many of these men's views have changed since those beginning days and they do not interfere.

Furthermore, the impact of the Rural Design School project extends to new generations. The elders saw a new the role women could play; girls grew up in an atmosphere where their opinions and ideas were acknowledged. As young adults, these girls understand the value of creativity, self-expression and integrity associated with their embroidery. Anjali says, "There have been small changes in a place where the culture hasn't changed in hundreds of years, and that's significant."

A Blueprint Worth Safekeeping

Today, if you were to walk through the village hamlet of Gandhi Nu Gaam, you would pass the well that provides water for all sixteen families in the village. You would see the *mandir* (temple) that rises above the *bhungas* that stand proudly in the heat. If you stayed the night, you would see a crystal clear canopy of stars above. Each morning you would hear the sounds of village life lived daily: the echoes of morning prayers from the temple, the bleating of goats as they are milked, and the crackling of burning wood feeding the *chulhas* (small, open-air stoves) for the day's first cup of *chai*. If you were to come to Gandhi Nu Gaam, you may notice the intentionality of each action and each day. You would bear witness to a community that has come together after seeing their surroundings come crashing down.

For Ludiya, the calamity of 2001 brought immense uncertainty and damage. Yet beyond the disaster and relief efforts emerged a new community of new capability. In 2008, the women self-organized and entered into an agreement with Gramshree, lending their talent to help create distinct pieces marketable to urban consumers. This relationship has allowed for a steady flow of work into Ludiya and surrounding villages, though many women say it is still not enough.

Perhaps the greatest lesson learned is the manner in which both Manav Sadhna and Indicorps engaged. The process of full investment into the lives of Ludiya went beyond any project plans or timelines. In the aftermath of tragedy, the emphasis was always about empowering a community that would eventually stand on its own — physically, economically, and with mindful togetherness. Since nature's fury is unlikely to abate, Ludiya's resurrection provides a blueprint for humanity's response.

OPERATION KHAZANA

The Treasure Within

In 2002, Krishnan Unnikrishnan joined Indicorps' inaugural class to pursue his theatrical passions through a year of service. A Harvard graduate who had dabbled in theatre in college, Krishnan wrote and directed a musical, Operation Khazana, through a collaborative process with his Mumbai-based partner organization Akanksha. Krishnan's vision for the musical mirrored Akanksha's larger objective to empower disadvantaged youth. Empowerment transpired on a number of levels: through the production process and the children's realization of a goal, via the take-away for the audience, and inwardly for Krishnan himself.

T he power of the arts is that it ignites the creative spark that allows us to dream of a better tomorrow. The power of service is that it takes us on a journey that requires us to re-examine what we want from ourselves and the world around us. The ability of each to take us down less-travelled paths has the power to change lives. Stories in particular, whether real or fictional, lend the inspiration to see the world anew.

In 2002, Krishnan Unnikrishnan joined Indicorps' inaugural Fellowship class expecting to pursue his theatrical passions through a year of service. Krishnan's year in India changed his life dramatically, as he eclipsed his own expectations. A graduate from Harvard with a pre-med background, Krishnan wrote and directed the musical, *Operation Khazana* for his Mumbai-based partner organization, Akanksha.

Operation Khazana was a 75-minute production. It involved over 180 children, as actors, dancers, chorus singers, backstage hands, and set creators. The preparation of the play, from creation to execution, lasted six months, beginning in September 2002. Over 800 children auditioned. Rehearsals and practices continued three times a week until the first performance in February 2003. Over the next several months, the musical was performed seven times in 2003 in Mumbai and Pune for audiences at some of the most prestigious venues in the city, including Nehru Auditorium in the Worli area of Mumbai. In total, the children of *Operation Khazana* performed on various stages for over 6,800 people.

The Story

Following a raggedy treasure map (the kind right out of a pirate story), Darshan, Tanushree and their friends set off on a quest in hopes of saving their beloved, yet bankrupt community center. Their quest is accompanied by dramatic music, epic fights scenes in front of flashing strobe lights, and choreographed dance sequences straight out of popular music videos. Each scene comes alive to the familiar sounds of both Bollywood hits and Western music including *The Lion King*, Michael Jackson, and *Phantom of the Opera*.

Amidst vibrant sets and captivating lighting, the children face many dangers which teach them how to conquer their own fears. When Darshan, Tanushree and company finally reach the treasure chest, instead of gold and jewels, they find the Ghost of Manu. To the tune of the Beatles' *Hey Jude*, the Ghost of Manu informs the group that the treasures they seek lay within them. The gang returns home perplexed and deflated. Suddenly, Darshan realizes the power to save the center is in their hands. Re-inspired, the crew puts together a play about their adventure and raises enough money from ticket sales to save the center.

The plot mirrored reality. Through this year-long adventure, many of the individuals involved — including Krishnan — recognized their own hidden strengths, talents, and passions and acted upon them.

The Cast

Mohar Ali, who played the role of Darshan, was one of Akanksha's earliest students and a member of the drama club. "I was very nervous during *Operation Khazana*. It was the first time I had ever performed in front of anyone, let alone a full audience," he admits. Mohar still lives in the same two-room, two-story shack behind

Akanksha
www.akanksha.org

With more than 50 centers and six schools, Akanksha focuses on creating a positive learning experience, self esteem, values, and a higher standard of living. Akanksha began as a supplementary education center with 15 children from a slum in Mumbai. Akanksha now reaches thousands of students annually. In 2002, Akanskha added theater as a creative learning tool into its curriculum to provide children with new opportunities to grow.

JOURNEY *Krishnan Unnikrishnan challenged the Operation Khazana cast to create meaning for both the audience and themselves by embodying the spirit of the production.*

the Mahalaxmi Race Course with his family of seven. Out the back window of the second-story room, only big enough to fit a mattress, is a brazen view of the horse stables. Mohar's family relocated to Mumbai from Bangladesh after their entire village was wiped out in a flood; Mohar was two years old. With no home and no placeto go, his family lived underneath a bridge begging for money. He spent his childhood days sneaking into the race grounds to play cricket.

Since *Operation Khazana*, Mohar has acted in two more Akanksha plays, and was a dancer featured in a documentary film. Mohar, 24, is employed as an experienced catering staffer and supplements his family's income. He is always on the lookout for another opportunity to display his artistic talents and credits Akanksha and *Operation Khazana* for the strength to support his family.

Sangeeta Zonbade, who played the role of Tanushree, was only 16 at the time of *Operation Khazana*. The youngest daughter in a single-parent household, Sangeeta grew up in a dangerous neighborhood.

In the early 1990s, she joined Akanksha as a student despite her family's hesitation. As one of nearly 900 children who auditioned for *Operation Khazana*, and with no previous acting experience, Sangeeta did not expect the play to have such a lasting impression. *Operation Khazana* serves as an important place marker in her own development.

"The impact [*Operation Khazana* had] on me was that I believed in myself. I could do it. I actually struggled a lot, which I have forgotten because we succeeded. But even now, that show gives me motivation that I can do things." Today at 24, Sangeeta jointly runs Akanksha's Social Leadership Program, an initiative aimed at building leadership in highly-motivated youth. Sangeeta is a strong, independent woman who supports her mother and remains confident in her own abilities and future.

Devdas Narayan Sripati, the Ghost of Manu, a once-regular at the Akanksha center in Mumbai's Worli district, has a bachelor's degree in commerce and is currently considering applying for his MBA. In his childhood, Devdas was bursting with energy throughout Akanksha classes. While his enthusiasm propelled his participation, his non-stop laughter and classroom antics were often a distraction. Many fondly recall Devdas' wit and found his optimism infectious.

Operation Khazana was Devdas' first play. Since then, he has performed in over three dozen productions. Devdas remembers Akanksha's drama classes and countless rehearsals: "I was not punctual I will be frank, but I always would attend. I had never done anything like that before. I didn't even realize what I was doing. It wasn't until a year later [after Khazana] that I even understood what I had done." These days, Devdas manages a Big Bazaar (a popular chain of grocery stores in India modeled after Wal-Mart), and is contemplating a stint in the Persian Gulf. As one of the eldest siblings, he contributes three-fourths of his income to support his family.

Even Krishnan's own journey captures the essence of *Operation Khazana*. Starting as the son of a doctor pursuing a pre-med degree at Harvard, he has become a film-maker launching films at festivals across the globe. "I probably wouldn't have gone to film school if it wasn't for that year," reflects Krishnan. "Through Indicorps, I was able to consciously choose how I wished to live and how I wished the world to be. What you live is what gets passed on to generations beyond."

The Show Must Go On

The idea of putting on a musical was something that Akanksha had always sought to do. Shaheen Mistry, founder and former CEO of Akanksha explains, "The dream of doing a musical had always been there in my head. The arts can be so important in building confidence and teamwork amongst kids." Mistry describes the *Operation Khazana* process as "a lot of chaos." Through this chaos emerged a coherent, professional, and moving production.

Understandably, there were plenty of challenges along the way. Many of them stemmed from the mammoth task of trying to organize and manage over a hundred teenagers. Amused, Sangeeta recalls, "Discipline was an issue. We were teenagers then and it was hard for Unni *bhaiya* (Krishnan) to control all of us. We used to make fun of Unni *bhaiya* a lot. His Hindi wasn't all that great so we used to say whatever we wanted, [and] he wouldn't know." Other challenges the production faced include: the children memorizing both English and Hindi lines, coordinating rehearsals with teams from multiple centers, and balancing everyday priorities with a finite timeline.

"What was really nice is what continued after [*Operation Khazana*]," shares Mistry. On the heels of *Operation Khazana's* tremendous success, Akanksha has organized musicals on a regular basis. They have run two more shows: *Once Upon a Time in Shantipur*, based on *Fiddler on the Roof*, and *Kabir and the Rangila Kurta*, based on *Joseph and the Technicolor Dream Coat*. The musicals have successfully weaved the arts with education in a nuanced manner that achieved Akanksha's dream of empowerment.

The Treasure is Within

Krishnan's vision for the musical paralleled Akanksha's larger social objectives. Most immediately, the play sought to empower youth by building confidence within them. In addition, the script was written to provoke critical thought. Krishnan says, "I took all the social norms and flipped them." For example, one scene featured a dominant matriarch who had enslaved the male population. The play also touched upon communal harmony and the larger pursuit of happiness. On opening night, Nehru Auditorium connected a cross-section of Mumbai society. Literally and metaphysically, the production of *Operation Khazana* challenged the children to re-define what they placed value on in life, as well as the audience's perspectives. Devdas says, "[The play] was not about money. It was about people's hearts. It was a message to change people's minds."

Operation Khazana added depth to the participants' perspective. "The most important thing about the play is the message. The real treasure is within," Mohar said. With a stone-cold serious look on his face, he insisted, "You can go looking for your dollars, but you'll never find any real treasure that way." The depth is certainly striking. These Akanksha youth who are upwardly mobile, yet still living in the slums, acknowledge that happiness does not come from external wealth.

For some, the process of putting on the play was the real production. Prashant Dodke, an Akanksha alumnus-turned-social worker and an actor in *Operation Khazana*, states, "I realized the journey of putting on the musical is the message of the play. The talents of dance and drama always existed in the students, but had to be found."

For those who saw their patronage as charity, this show revealed a new source of talent. Mansi Sanghvi, a teacher and drama club coordinator with Akanksha chuckled, "I think people were stunned and shocked to see that kids from these backgrounds could be a part of something so big. The audience couldn't believe the talent they witnessed, because generally that talent remains untapped."

While many Akanskha students have been able to translate their experiences into self-confidence, good jobs and familial responsibility, others still struggle to find employment and fulfill their own potential. Money is a continuous problem that Devdas says will never end: "Things are really bad here. Today there are so many problems. It still embarrasses me that we don't have proper access to water where I live." Despite such hardships, Devdas radiates positivity that suggests maturity exceeding his 23 years.

The personal and collective transformation in Mohar, Sangeeta, Devdas, Krishnan and the *Operation Khazana* troupe demonstrates the richness that comes from deliberate adventuring. It is not Sangeeta's near-flawless English, or Devdas' uninhibited articulation of his fears and frustrations, hopes and dreams that is most striking. Rather, it is the values each of these young adults holds that is both inspiring and humbling.

Epilogue

Over four brief days in Mumbai, I traversed the city from the slums of Bandra, to the Millennium Mall in Worli, to the Akanksha office in Chinchpokli in an attempt to decipher the continuing impact of *Operation Khazana*. Physically, many of the circumstances are the same. However, the players' themselves have evolved. I suppose this is the transformative nature of both the arts and service. While critics may fail to see how one play can have such a meaningful impact, the *Operation Khazana* journey continues to exemplify how stories can be catalysts for change.

As Mohar and I passed by the entrance to the Mahalaxmi Race Course, he stopped me. "*Bhaiya*, when I was little, I used to come here and beg for money." We continued onwards across the street for a cup of *chai*. Mohar insisted on paying. He then accompanied me to the bus stand to ensure I caught the right bus home.

Mohar's journey. The message of *Operation Khazana*. The promise of tomorrow's potential. If I had to make a treasure map, "X" would mark this spot. These are treasures worth searching for.

Pulse of the People

In 2005, Christina Mathews partnered with Bhoruka Charitable Trust to address issues of maternal and child health in rural Rajasthan. Christina's full immersion into the communities taught her the value of grassroots service to shape lives as well as policies. Being a part of the change in India has shaped her professional contributions in Rhode Island, Lesotho and Boston; it has also reinforced Christina's commitment to living her values.

Christina Mathews, 30, has crossed continents, boundaries, and cultures in the pursuit of improving public health. Born in Dallas, Texas, the third child of Malayali Christian immigrants, Christina had limited interaction with India after living in Kerala with her grandparents for the first four years of her life. Christina has always had a sincere passion for service. From a very young age she used to voice how she wanted "to help people in developing countries." At each major milestone in her life, that passion and desire only grew more and more.

The Indicorps Fellowship catalyzed Christina to live life outside conventional lines and pursue a unique brand of service. Throughout her career, the lines have encompassed profound experiences. In 2010, Christina wrote a long-term, training curriculum for community health workers in the Nilgiri Hills of Tamil Nadu, India. In 2007, she collaborated with the Health Ministry of Lesotho to improve the infrastructure of government hospitals and to assess the brain drain of health professionals from Lesotho. From 2007-09, Christina coordinated the tobacco control policy agenda for the Rhode Island Department of Health in the United States. In addition, she put her grassroots experiences to good use as an advocate on behalf of global poverty as she chaired the CARE Action Network state chapter.

Christina's approach to public health and her philosophy of social service, inspired by Indicorps, distinguish her experiences. As a 2005 Indicorps Fellow paired with Bhoruka Charitable Trust (BCT), Christina journeyed to the Rajasthani desert to address severe maternal and child health problems of malnutrition and infant mortality. Christina arrived in the village of Bhorugram with a Masters degree in International Public Health from Boston University.

The intensity of her time on the ground in Rajasthan made a deep impact on Christina, which has shaped her subsequent public health endeavors. Pushing herself to immerse in a community that was radically foreign to her, living her values and ideals in a conservative culture, and embracing uncertainty — all informed her way of being. "In one word, the impact on my life [from my Indicorps year in Rajasthan] was that it gave me a sense of fearlessness. That is something that stays with me everyday since my time in Bhorugram. That year was the beginning of a long-term commitment to India, but also to global public health work as a whole."

Pulse of the People

When Christina arrived in Bhorugram, the situation was dire — approximately 40 to 45 children under the age of two were dying each month. Malnutrition, various communicable diseases, poor maternal health, and risky home deliveries all contributed to such an alarming mortality rate. Christina was tasked with the broad mandate of decreasing infant mortality. Through increased government cooperation and intense village-level interventions, BCT has carried forward Christina's efforts and successfully lowered the infant mortality rate in the Bhorugram vicinity from 53 deaths to 46 deaths per 1,000 births. The interventions focused on improving breastfeeding practices, ensuring close monitoring of pregnant women, early treatment of children with diarrhea and other infections, and increased vaccination rates. BCT maintains a

Bhoruka Charitable Trust
www.bctngo.org

Established in 1962 in the village of Bhorugram, Rajasthan, Bhoruka Charitable Trust (BCT) focuses on the social and economic transformation of rural India. BCT's holistic approach extends to health, education, infrastructure development, natural resource management, and disaster mitigation. BCT has geographically expanded remote regions of Rajasthan, Karnataka, Andhra Pradesh, Maharashtra, and Port Blair. BCT supports existing government initiatives such as the Integrated Child Development Services program for maternal and child health services.

RESPECT *Christina Mathews' experience in Bhorugram was defined by the relationships she built with people like Kitobaji, the cleaning lady, who greeted Christina as a returned daughter upon her re-visit in 2009.*

database in which every pregnant woman in the Bhorugram vicinity is monitored. Furthermore, BCT operates the government's Integrated Child Development Services program in five districts of the state, and provides curative health services through mobile clinic vans and its own hospital.

Following Indicorps' "look, listen, and learn" protocol, Christina spent her first six weeks at BCT fully immersing and shadowing women in the community. "I would go where they were. I went to the fields to harvest *bajra* with the women. If they were collecting water at the well at 5 am, I would go there. I spent time at the local school with the kids and teachers. I developed relationships, which strengthened me personally and my project throughout the year. This initial immersion period was very useful in getting a feel for the pulse of the community."

While Christina arrived with an action plan, her project evolved many times during her Fellowship year. She tested a number of ideas in the early months. Christina began by creating health clubs for adolescent girls. She tried improving pre-school education at the local *anganwadi* centers (government pre-schools). Ultimately, Christina decided to further develop a new BCT initiative, and build the capacity of the newly appointed *Sahayoginis* in each village. The *Sahayoginis*, appointed as part of a state government initiative to address high malnutrition rates, were tasked with educating and supporting pregnant and breastfeeding women in their village.

Christina and a BCT field worker began the project by administering a survey to pregnant and breastfeeding women in the area to get a baseline of current practices. They would visit neighboring villages by motorcycle, bus or camel cart to understand what feeding practices in Rajasthan might be contributing to the high malnutrition rates. Christina witnessed mothers, believing that it was better for the baby, provide animal milk to infants the day they were born. She intently listened to new mothers discussing treatments for diarrhea and

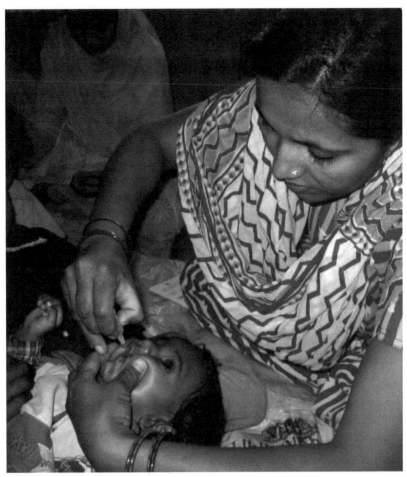

EMBRACE *In addition to counseling mothers on breastfeeding and post-natal care, Sahayoginis (woman health workers) meticulous ly provide hundreds of infants in villages with polio vaccine.*

pneumonia, common causes for infant deaths. In these discussions, Christina observed the strong role mothers-in-law played in the lives of their daughters-in-law and in caring for the newborn babies.

From simple motivation to providing on-the-job-training, Christina's role in strengthening *Sahayoginis'* capabilities ranged dramatically. In the conservative climate of rural Rajasthan, she regularly coaxed *Sahayoginis* to embrace their responsibilities as village health workers. "The purpose of the *Sahayogini* is to counsel pregnant and breastfeeding women. Yet, many were unable to even leave their homes. Just trying to get women out of the house was often a chore. I spent a lot of time talking to [*Sahayoginis'*] mothers-in-law. There were huge negotiations with their mothers-in-law to let them go [on their home visits]. I would try and explain the problem of malnutrition in our villages and the fact that kids were dying every day and that their daughters-in-law could have an immense impact in preventing this from happening," Christina recalls.

Christina would accompany *Sahayoginis* on their house visits and provide training on the spot, in real time. She also conducted group trainings at local government health centers. Based upon the findings of the survey, Christina developed a breastfeeding counseling module — with creative and participatory activities — to raise awareness in villages. Christina created a framework of best practices that the *Sahayoginis* and she employed on regular home visits. Naroma Nayakar, a government health worker in Hansivas, a village nearby Bhorugram, remembers, "[Christina] brought women together and provided a lot of education on health. She used to organize games between women and from these games they would learn a lot about their own health and what they could do in the field."

As one of the few women who would openly show her face in a *purdah* (veiled) society, Christina held a unique position in the BCT villages. She formed bonds with women, attempted to understand their mores, and collaborated to improve the health of the village. Christina found that despite coming from such different backgrounds, she had much in common with the *Sahayoginis*. "In essence, we were both trying to do the same thing. We were both doing something that was out of our comfort zone with a lot of external challenges. There was solidarity in that," Christina explains.

The Christina Standard

The emphasis Indicorps placed on service as a transformative experience shaped Christina's learnings in a profound way. Christina discovered that personal, professional, and societal transformation is indeed intertwined. "Feeling the scorching summer heat, carrying water in *matkas* to my building, waking up to the peacocks crowing allowed me to experience a beautiful connectivity with the earth. I was able to see how actions of one person can reverberate around the world and experience how the policies of one country can shape the global landscape."

Christina brought her own passion, knowledge, and drive to the already well-established activities at BCT. As one of BCT's first international volunteers, Christina set a precedent for what dedicated, young people can add to rural development. BCT Executive Director Amitav Banerjee says, "[Christina] brought determination and passion. She built a good rapport with the community. She initiated the training program with the *Sahayoginis* and her training skills were excellent."

Since 2006, BCT has established links with international voluntary agencies and currently takes on volunteers from places as diverse as Peru, Switzerland, and Korea. "The Christina Standard" opened doors for others to enrich and be enriched by dedicated service at BCT. Banerjee credits Christina for creating a strong platform: "Christina started this interest in working with international interns and volunteers."

Rajasthan Remained Relevant

Post-fellowship Christina brought the fearlessness, adaptability, and grassroots immersion from her Indicorps field experience to other professional arenas. Christina has been able to transfer her learnings from her time in Rajasthani villages into practical, policy recommendations in both India and around the world. Immediately after her time with BCT, Christina remained in Rajasthan to continue addressing malnutrition issues. For three months she partnered with UNICEF as they set up malnutrition treatment centers across the state.

Christina's ability to see the potential of impacting communities from both the policy and grassroots level has allowed her new insights. "I saw the ground realities of action plans drafted in boardrooms around the world. I saw that often well-intentioned policies were lost in translation when administered in local communities," Christina says.

In Rhode Island, Christina tackled tobacco control policy with the Department of Health. In this radically different setting, Rajasthan remained relevant. Christina's beginnings in advocacy with mothers-in-law in Bhorugram provided insightful perspective as she wrote testimony for the state on the power dynamics between the tobacco industry and local poor and minority communities.

Christina says, "Lessons learned during the Fellowship have been immensely helpful in my work since. The 'look, listen, and learn' mantra has become the way in which I approach new people and new scenarios. During my Fellowship, we were encouraged to problem solve creatively as new challenges continued to arise; I approached my work at the state health department in the same way." Christina succeeded in helping introduce 12 tobacco control bills during the legislative session, while cultivating relationships with community-based organizations. Christina dealt with contentious debates and "very heated meetings" between community partners. She says, "I quickly saw how little listening was really happening and tried to listen as much as possible."

Even after various positions in administrative settings, she has made a point to stay attuned to the realities on the ground. Christina's commitment to service and India brought her back to this homeland once again. In 2009, newly-wed, she returned to India with her husband Nick, an ophthalmologist. Christina and Nick devoted six months to preventive and curative health issues in South India. Christina developed a training curriculum with the Association for Health Welfare in the Nilgiris (ASHWINI), a 2008 Indicorps' partner organization, while Nick worked with a local doctor to conduct cataract surgery and eye camps in remote areas. Christina and Nick also made a special visit to Bhorugram. It was particularly important for Christina to share her India, through social service, with Nick.

Nick says, "Our time volunteering together in India was rewarding beyond words, as it gave me just a glimpse of the passion for service and discovery that was ignited in Christina during her time as an Indicorps Fellow. It was wonderful to visit Bhorugram to put the smiling faces to the myriad of stories from her year there. Watching Kitaboji, the cleaning woman for the BCT office, burst with pride as she clutched Christina tightly for more than ten minutes and jokingly scolded herself for letting her daughter [Christina] go, I saw in full circle the effects of this deep human connection. It was amazing."

Christina's older sister Regina adds, "Indicorps enriched our family through Christina's experiences, and continues to do so, with an increased desire for service and change in all of us... Just hearing about her interactions with the women and children in Bhorugram made us realize it was possible to make an impact on a huge level, starting with a small village in Rajasthan."

Connecting Bhorugram to Boston and Beyond

Christina is in the midst of organizing a number of projects that she directly correlates to her days in the desert. Her Indicorps' experience has allowed her to connect seemingly disparate dots in her career with kaleidoscopic lines. Christina connected Bhorugram to Boston, where in 2004 she was involved in breast cancer research at Massachusetts General Hospital. In 2010, Christina asked the Bhorugram women in veils to reconfigure their fabric designs to make head scarves for women in Boston undergoing chemotherapy. The project is one part income generation, and one part connectivity. The essence of exchange goes beyond monetary benefits.

Christina says, "This project came out of the solidarity I felt with the women of Bhorugram and the women I worked with in Boston. The aim is to create headscarves for cancer patients in the U.S., share India's beautiful textile arts, and use organic fabrics to convey the stories of women across borders." For Christina, a Herman Melville quote captures the essence: "We cannot live for ourselves alone, our lives are connected by a thousand invisible threads, and along these sympathetic fibers our actions run as causes and return to us as results."

In the Indicorps spirit, Christina's journey embodies a constant re-drawing of the lines to stretch the boundaries of human connection and human potential. In Christina's world, boundaries continue to dissolve in both a personal and professional capacity. From the Bhorugram government hospital to the Rhode Island State House, from drinking *chai* with Kitaboji to sipping herbal tea with policymakers, Christina does not let the setting define what is possible. As each experience informs the next, Christina strives to remain the evolving constant by living her values, fearlessly.

Living the
Alternative

In January 2007, Fellow Rohan Jasani traded in electrical engineering, consulting and break-dancing for a year with Sampoorna Bamboo Kendra in the Melghat Forest. Living in one of Indicorps' most remote project sites, Rohan shared his knowledge in design, marketing, and production. Through his own example, he inspired confidence in the bamboo artisans to incorporate creative experimentation into their craft practices and to exceed their own perceived limitations. Rohan found an alignment with the tribal way of life, which shape his decisions to this day.

The flick of the knife splits stalk after hollow stalk. Beams of light stream through the thatched roof. The hum of saws and drills hangs over the constant chatter of tribal languages. In the *adivasi* village of Lawada, in the Melghat Forest, people have journeyed from all over the region to congregate inside the workshop, amongst the floating sawdust. Here, artisans are trained to create crafts, furniture, and houses — all from the renewable resource of bamboo.

In Lawada, there is an inherent belief in living congruently with the natural surroundings. Sampoorna Bamboo Kendra (SBK) consciously endeavors to impart craftsmanship skills that are environmentally-responsible, culturally-aware, and applicable to procuring a steady income. Bamboo is one of nature's strongest resources; SBK's homegrown philosophy is possibly even stronger. In the face of rapid modernization, SBK presents a holistic alternative that integrates craft and construction, artisanship and learning, and people's connection to the earth. "What we believe in is bringing justice to three things — man, materials, and methodology," says Sunil Deshpande, SBK co-founder and managing director.

At age 27, Rohan Jasani left his job at a top-tier technology consulting firm to explore rural India through a year of intense service. "I came to India to pursue other aspects of my being. I came to reconnect with nature, simplify my life, and further develop my creative passions through service," says Rohan. As an Indicorps Fellow, Rohan partnered with SBK, boosting their efforts to provide rural livelihoods. He adopted many facets of the organization's approach which improved the design and production of bamboo crafts, furniture and housing. Rohan also experimented with different techniques to make the process more efficient. Over a year of successes and failures, Rohan contributed significant input on the treatment of bamboo products, the training process of artisans and instructors, and the final production of goods. As he absorbed the culture of the organization and the people of the Melghat Forest into his daily lifestyle, Rohan became part of the local community.

Early Struggles

Rohan began to understand that finding employment was one of the biggest challenges facing Lawada. In the Melghat Forest most men migrate to nearby cities to find jobs anywhere between six to eight months a year. Historically, the *adivasi* communities fulfilled their daily needs from the forest. They then shifted to sustenance farming and later almost exclusively to cash crops. The ability to live a self-sustained existence has been lost. High instances of child malnutrition have only made the situation grimmer. At its core, SBK re-connects this indigenous society to a country that is rapidly changing. As Rohan states, "The tribal youth of the Melghat shout on behalf of all rural youth across India, 'Employ me not in the city, but in the rural setting of my home.' The truth is what they echo, not some analytical perspective from the outside."

While Lawada has limited electricity, many interior villages of the Melghat still do not. People not only lack access to running water, they do not even have the money to build wells. Agriculture suffers as there is no irrigation. The people of the Melghat Forest must confront a harsh reality, one that seems incomprehensible from the outside.

Sampoorna Bamboo Kendra

Sampoorna Bamboo Kendra (SBK) provides livelihood opportunities to surrounding *adivasi* (tribal) communities already well-versed in bamboo craft. Officially established in 1997, SBK operates a training center in Lawada and eight satellite centers in neighboring villages. SBK trains local villagers on how to design, build, price, and market bamboo products for external markets. SBK presents some of the artisans' products at the Lawada center and at exhibitions across the country. Moreover, it advocates for artisans' rights and the widespread use of bamboo.

Living the Alternative

ACHIEVE The SBK workshop provides an opportunity for community members to generate a livelihood by developing their own skills using bamboo, a renewable resource.

When Rohan first arrived in Lawada, and entered through SBK's bamboo gate, he struggled. "The first couple months were rocky," he remembers. With virtually no understanding of Hindi, and absolutely no comprehension of the local *adivasi* languages, verbal communication was limited. Rohan also survived regular electricity cuts, daily trips to the well, ice-cold buckets baths, and a wide collection of insects and critters sharing the floor where he slept. "Everyone had this thing. They would say, 'You're just this kid from America.' They didn't think I was going to last."

Nearly every single person at SBK recalls those days well and has stories about Rohan's early struggles. Everyone also proudly remarked on the effort Rohan made in understanding the local culture and becoming a part of the community. "Most people [who visit SBK] leave in a week or two. I think the fact that I was able to stick it out had an impact on people." With Rohan's mentorship, Chanda Dharwa, an SBK organizer, developed a spirit of exploration and outpaced her peers. She drew inspiration from Rohan's full immersion: "Rohan was someone who gave so much effort, who applied his mind so fully," she says.

Fair Trade Lifestyle

Within weeks Rohan traded in his baggy jeans and buttoned-down shirt for a lungi; his hip-hop-infused slang for the local blend of Hindi and Korku dialect; and most importantly, his endorsement of a fair trade seal for a fair trade lifestyle. He lived in solidarity with the artisans, seeking greater equity through dialogue, transparency and mutual respect. Rohan's dedication seemed to complement the Deshpandes' vision of bringing honor, respect and justice to artisans, and of promoting the virtues of bamboo. SBK's sustainable practices emphasize an understanding of and reliance on the resources indigenous to India. "Our vision is a very big one. It involves India embracing its own philosophy [to tackle its challenges] instead of following others," says Sunil Deshpande.

At SBK, bamboo is not simply viewed as an instrumental material, it is respected and revered. Understandably, every structure at the Lawada center from the furniture and accessories, to the main workshop, to the Deshpandes' home is made from bamboo. Deshpande's belief in the potential of bamboo is just as much about the usefulness of the plant, as it is about justice. He believes that all materials, including bamboo, should be used to their full capacity.

For over 15 years, SBK has provided job skills for hundreds of individuals in the Melghat Forest. While many who come to Lawada already work with bamboo as part of their cultural tradition, SBK training allows them to create more diverse and intricate products. Despite operating in such an isolated environment, SBK has forged partnerships with the State Forest Department and the Indira Gandhi National Open University (IGNOU) to provide incentives and academic certification. In addition, SBK has supported the formation of over 200 micro-finance Self Help Groups in the Melghat area, helping communities strengthen their own economic footing.

The organization also provides a space for hands-on learning. After receiving training from SBK, villagers go back to their homes and make their own goods, either selling them directly, or bringing them back to Lawada for the organization to market on their behalf. Along with the opportunity to learn experientially in the bamboo workshop, villagers attend daily lectures that Deshpande provides on topics such as the anatomy of bamboo, pricing strategy, and how to innovate and create. The sessions he leads are both didactic and hilarious. As a geometry teacher, accountant, and stand-up comedian Deshpande makes people feel they want to be there. Between lectures, artisans lend their voices in traditional song and prayer towards progress.

Jigs and Fixtures

With an understanding of Deshpande's philosophy, Rohan also saw the power of incorporating the local culture in bamboo craftwork and design. For example, Rohan adapted the tattoo designs that many elderly women had on their arms onto greeting cards. In addition to innovating card designs, Rohan experimented with the look of SBK's wide array of bamboo products including furniture, mats, and household accessories. By applying his own background in engineering and visual arts, Rohan suggested improvements that aided both production and marketing. A simple change in the shape of bamboo trivets dramatically improved the aesthetic and allowed for the trivets to be transported and sold in greater quantity. Rohan helped regulate the process of improvement by introducing a quality checklist, and implemented the use of an efficiency-enhancing intervention known as "jigs and fixtures." These improvements increased the speed and quality of production. Rohan also utilized his photography talent to document SBK's efforts. His photographs drove a branding and marketing campaign that generated pamphlets, certificates, posters and product catalogs. Eventually, he launched the SBK website.

Rohan also played a key role in developing trainings on housing and handicrafts. While basic trainings had been on-going for some time, Rohan assisted in putting together two of SBK's first set of advanced trainings — Advanced Bamboo Housing Training and Advanced Bamboo Craft Teachers Training, which was specifically aimed at training instructors. Rohan created easily replicable models to train teachers. A consistent blueprint provided the guidance for artisans to efficiently improve their own output. Furthermore, training more teachers extended the craft to more artisans.

"Leveraging the quality control system I created may have been one of the greatest contributions of these trainings, as it was used as the metric for testing knowledge and skill. It allowed us to formalize the evaluation process of trainees' bamboo artisan skills, a hard thing to measure," says Rohan.

Rohan's own knowledge of bamboo grew as he familiarized himself with each product. Experimentation through trial and error became almost a daily task. On his own, Rohan tried over 40 different methods to treat bamboo to protect it from fungi, termites and other insects. He collaborated with artisans diligently and experimented with traditional, eco-friendly varnishes, powders, and even boiled saltwater to improve the lifespan and durability of the bamboo products. Rohan succeeded and failed many times during his experimentation with structural design and treatment.

"[My efforts] constantly drove home the message that failure is necessary to succeed and that it is okay to fail. Watching my struggles lessened my counterparts' fear of trying things out [and] allowed them to give it their all. My attention to detail and quality, as well as my standard for excellence, also sent a strong message. My perspectives on design, engineering and art expanded the scope of technical and creative boundaries, and boosted their confidence as artisans," Rohan recalls.

Outside of trainings, experimentation, and exhibitions, Rohan intermittently tried to teach dance classes in Lawada, using his own artistic passion as a way to further connect with the community. He helped run regular morning yoga sessions and screened films to help develop life-skills amongst the local *adivasi* population. From break-dancing to Bollywood, Rohan used dance and laughter to bridge the cultural gap.

Purposeful and Principal Living

Rohan's immense personal learnings offset his contribution to SBK for a mutual windfall. "I've learned as much from SBK, the founders, staff, artisans and the community as they have from me. Seeing how Sunil *bhau* and Nirupama *tai* live strengthened my own confidence to live my values and contribute positively to the world. I learned about sticking to something I believe in. I was able to transfer these ideas

I always had into a practical lifestyle I could live and take with me beyond Lawada," says Rohan.

Since his days in the Melghat Forest, Rohan has blended the purposeful and principled living he discovered at SBK with his professional career as head of user interface design at a software company in the United States. He chose to live in an intentional community to help cultivate a more socially-conscious lifestyle. Based on his own study of *ayurvedic* principles, Rohan is deliberate about his intake. He does not drink alcohol, embraced vegetarianism, planted a 300-square foot organic garden with over 40 varieties of medicinal herbs and vegetables, and incorporated *vipassana* meditation into his daily practice, after attending several ten day silent meditation retreats. He also made time to spearhead pro-bono service projects for Indicorps and various other social initiatives.

Rohan found that his experiments in living congruently with his surroundings, inspired by his Fellowship year, allowed him to re-new the most valuable of resources — a commitment to the pursuit of personal truth.

Mind Your Business

In 2007, Fellow Naveen Lakshmipathy swapped a prestigious advocacy job in Washington DC for small scale rural infrastructure development in the Hubli-Dharwad region of Karnataka. Naveen partnered with the Small Scale Sustainable Infrastructure Development Fund (S³IDF) to increase accessibility to clean energy through alternative business models. Focusing on biogas in dairy villages and LED-powered lights for urban street hawkers, Naveen's approach revealed the value of business solutions that keep the community at the center.

In 2007, Naveen Lakshmipathy embarked on a two-year rollercoaster journey that took him to crowded marketplaces of Dharwad, Karnataka and surrounding farming villages. Naveen journeyed to India intending to harness the power of the marketplace to promote social change. With an affinity for business and an analytical mind frame, his focus was on achieving clear and measurable results. The unique three-way partnership between Indicorps, the Small Scale Sustainable Infrastructure Development Fund (S³IDF), and Naveen facilitated a process that combined grassroots organizing with market-based solutions. Through several infrastructure development campaigns, Naveen quickly learned that business as usual would not work.

The story begins with Naveen's journey to India as an August 2007 Indicorps Fellow. Though he eventually gained the support of his family, Naveen's choice to spend initially one, and ultimately two, years in rural India caused them great confusion and anxiety. Not only was he leaving a research and advocacy job at a respected think-tank in Washington DC, he was also risking missing his sister's wedding in order to plunge headfirst into the villages and marketplaces of Karnataka. In the end, the opportunity to join the growing sustainable business movement for community-centered change was too great to resist.

By facilitating community partnerships, S³IDF enables local entrepreneurs to provide improved infrastructure and energy services to the informal sector. S³IDF's approach stresses practical, environmentally- and financially-sustainable business models that place economic responsibility directly in ordinary people's hands. Naveen, Indicorps, and S³IDF shared the belief that learning from local people is essential to developing sustainable solutions.

S³IDF entrusted Naveen with the challenge of expanding its efforts to Hubli-Dharwad. As a result of Naveen's efforts, S³IDF's main focus in this new locale became promoting biogas energy, providing clean, reliable lighting to underserved communities, and ensuring access to a supply chain of eco-friendly appliances.

Naveen came to this project with experience in advocacy and a desire to initiate social change through business ventures. Most importantly, he poured his heart and soul into the project. "It was intimidating and exciting at the same time. I was armed with a few months of training, a broad mandate, and an anxiety to make something of my time. I had to figure out a game plan, and go for it," says Naveen. As the sole S³IDF representative on the ground in Dharwad, Naveen enabled collaborations between different stakeholders in various energy enterprises. "[Being in Dharwad] was a lot of relationship building, immersion, and overnight-stays in different communities. I was planting seeds that had no guarantee of flowering."

Through his training with Indicorps and S³IDF, Naveen cultivated the interpersonal and analytical tools that were essential for gathering information from the local community about how to improve basic infrastructure and energy services. Naveen reached out to local non-profits including Best Practices Foundation, NEEDS, Spoorty, and

Small Scale Sustainable Infrastructure Development Fund
www.s3idf.org

The Small Scale Sustainable Infrastructure Development Fund (S³IDF) is a non-profit organization that provides infrastructure and related services by facilitating finance, business development and technical services for poverty alleviation in India. S³IDF supplies infrastructure services using existing sources of small-scale finance. Projects include energy efficient lighting, energy, and stoves; supply chain and enterprise support; livelihoods and transportation. Originating in Southern Karnataka, S³IDF expanded to the regions around Dharwad and Hyderabad in 2007.

Mind Your Business

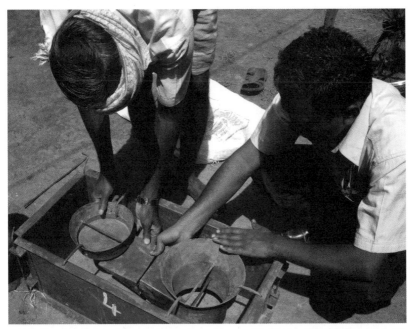

INNOVATE *A smokeless chulha (traditional stove) is assembled in the village of Nayakanahatti. Naveen Lakshmipathy, the S³IDF team, and their partners constantly sought to explore innovative solutions.*

HARNESS *Naveen Lakshmipathy joins hands with the people of Surshettykoppa to build the first ever biogas unit in the village.*

Vidya Poshak, and accompanied them into the field. Through this intense immersion and hands-on interaction, he developed a strong understanding of the daily lives, struggles, and aspirations behind the marketplace. He saw genuine strengths and identified potential gaps. Eventually, Naveen decided to focus on two critical infrastructure gaps: the need for clean, affordable fuel for cooking in rural areas, and the need for modern, efficient lighting solutions for urban street hawkers.

Naveen became acutely aware of the challenge many rural households faced in cooking, an activity that he had previously taken for granted. He realized that most families in the region had to collect or purchase wood and other fuels for cooking. Moreover, he learned that cooking on inefficient and smoke-emitting indoor stoves posed major health threats. Naveen became energized when he visited a handful of communities that had found an elegant solution to this problem: biogas technology. Biogas units, which can be constructed out of cement and brick, convert cow dung and other organic waste into safe, non-polluting energy. "It's a simple technology that's been around a long time, and a lot of people know about it, but they don't invest in it," says Naveen. "Many families own cattle, so they already have a source of clean renewable fuel, they just need the technology to harness it," he adds.

In order to promote access to biogas through a sustainable business model, Naveen began organizing with the Karnataka Milk Federation (KMF), a state-run cooperative of cattle farmers. Initially, he found great enthusiasm for a biogas initiative. However, after nearly six months of reaching out to village-level dairy cooperatives and structuring loan options for local farmers to build biogas units, the partnership with KMF failed due to administrative reasons. Naveen recollects, "I was disappointed [it did not work], but I realized the process was not in vain ... I learned that we needed a partner organization that could more easily integrate biogas awareness, loan disbursement, collection, and continuing support to families into the core work." Knowing better what he needed for success, it was here that Naveen recalls "hitting the reset button."

Naveen was determined to find another way to make biogas accessible for villagers. In a second attempt, he set up a partnership with BAIF Institute for Rural Development - Karnataka, an organization dedicated to sustainable rural development through agriculture and livelihood promotion. Together, Naveen and BAIF's community leaders devised a plan to give interest-free loans to families through a local lending co-op, Maha Sangha. With a plan in place, Naveen began regularly attending Maha Sangha community meetings in nearby villages.

As the S³IDF point-person, Naveen linked BAIF, local technicians, and the local government to construct the biogas units. In addition to arranging for interest-free loans, Naveen and S³IDF asked for sweat equity from the families to build ownership of the process. Ramamani Rao, S³IDF's Public Relations Manager explains, "Our business model recognizes [people's] ability to pay. The poor are already paying for unreliable and costly resources. Through biogas they are able to save, repay their loan, and save more."

Naveen patiently explained the benefits, cajoled, and motivated community members to invest in biogas. Rajendra Prasad Mugdal, a S³IDF field organizer acknowledges, "Naveen traveled a lot. He would attend meetings, identify community members [who were willing to build biogas units], convince people, and make follow-up visits. It was necessary to visit a minimum of three to five times [to convince families to adopt biogas]." This part of the process proved to be the toughest.

For Naveen and S³IDF, the impact was more than just access to clean, renewable energy; the odorless, sterile slurry byproduct is a potent organic fertilizer. Malappa Sivappa Kamadenu, a farmer in the village of Sursettykoppa who appreciates Naveen's contribution says, "Using biogas for cooking has saved us time and energy for other activities. We vermicompost the slurry. Adding it to our fields has improved yield."

In addition, Naveen's efforts positively impacted health. The use of biogas prevents harmful smoke inhalation and approximately 30-45 days per year of collecting firewood. Biogas user Laxmi Manikchand says, "I used to suffer from [inhaling] lots of smoke with the wood-fire *chulha*... In the rainy season it's hard to get dry firewood. Now there's no problem."

Even though he stood to gain nothing from the final transaction, Naveen's persistence was extraordinary. He found that families who initially expressed interest later backed out due to the fear of having to make a large investment. Only three out of ten people who first said they wanted a biogas unit followed through with the agreement. Some said they no longer had the money or space for a biogas unit. Others encouraged Naveen, who had traveled six hours roundtrip, to come back and speak to another family member the next day. The list of excuses became as innovative as the technology itself.

"I was frustrated by the slow pace of progress, but I could empathize with the hesitation many families faced. They understood the investment in biogas would provide them with clean, low-cost energy that would enable them to save money in the long run — they even knew of neighbors who had made the investment a decade earlier and been very happy — but the cost of the initial investment scared them away." The persistence required and timeframe for acceptance defied short-term profit-making. "I was convinced that momentum would eventually build, even if it took a very long time," Naveen recalls. Nearly a year after Naveen's departure, signs of progress began to show. When Naveen left Kamplikoppa village in July 2009, only one family was using biogas. In April 2010, there were eight.

On the urban front, Naveen invested heavily in community-oriented energy solutions for evening street hawkers in Dharwad's Nehru Market. Informal-sector vendors play a critical role in local economies throughout India, but most are severely underserved with respect to basic infrastructure. Many use makeshift stands or sit on tarps without light. Some rely on expensive, polluting kerosene lamps that endanger their health and generate heat and smoke that spoil edible wares. In 2005, S³IDF developed a business model to empower local entrepreneurs to rent out clean, low-cost, portable electric lights to street vendors on a nightly basis. The model was running successfully in several large markets in Bangalore. Naveen took on the challenge of adapting the model for Dharwad.

Once more, he experienced failures along the way. Naveen began the initiative by testing a battery-powered LED lantern for Rs. 10 per night with ten hawkers. Naveen invested hundreds of hours interacting with vendors, building camaraderie and trust, and physically distributing out the 12 kg batteries. After a few weeks, feedback from hawkers revealed that the new lights were not sufficiently bright or dependable. Naveen next piloted a more powerful CFL light/battery system for Rs. 15 per night. Feedback was positive, and the enterprise soon stabilized with over 20 customers.

Nishar Tamboli, a 25 year-old who runs a *paan* stand, recalls, "Everyday it cost me more to keep a kerosene lamp. A CFL light requires no maintenance. It's easy. [Naveen] said use it for free for a day. I have been using it ever since." Within a year of Naveen's departure, more than half of the 100 street hawkers in Nehru Market had switched to battery-powered lights provided by S³IDF, and other similar businesses were inspired by S³IDF's approach. As both a good business practice and sustainability measure, Naveen groomed a local salesman, Mr. Shankar, to organize the daily distribution, maintenance, and collection of the light systems. Mr. Shankar gradually took financial ownership of the business via a loan.

Naveen's social impact could easily be measured in units of clean energy supplied, in number of collaborations formed, or in local entrepreneurs empowered. However, for Naveen, the greatest impact of his time was not the change he helped drive in the community, but how the process of change changed him. From a business standpoint, spending long hours with street vendors may not seem efficient; however the resulting relationships and cultivated patience had long-term significance. Naveen says, "I used to be such a means-end person. I always felt like I was missing something. I was looking at the end goals of my actions, and believing that if X, Y, or Z happened, I would find happiness and satisfaction. I was looking at life the wrong way. I've realized now that it's the journey, the struggle that counts — that there is beauty and value to be found in every single moment along the way... Now, I am more engaged, and more in the present moment."

Business remains Naveen's forte. In fall 2010, Naveen began his MBA at the University of Michigan Ross School of Business. Naveen says, "My time in India got me energized about the potential for community-run sustainable businesses to generate economic opportunities and to be a force for social change. With 'social enterprise' being thrown around as a buzzword in business schools today, I believe my experience immersing in and working alongside communities to implement business solutions regarding infrastructure issues gives me invaluable perspective on what this really means." Naveen's continued commitment to market-based solutions, while embracing the nuances of the process, will make for a valuable journey beyond the bottom-line.

A Sanitation Awakening

In January 2008, Fellow Sowmya Somnath, a successful structural engineer, left her job and home for a year of grassroots service in Rehabilitation Colony #3 near Sindhanur, Karnataka. Partnered with Swami Vivekananda Youth Movement (SVYM), Sowmya brought an arsenal of diverse grassroots experiences to the refugee community. Sowmya aimed to improve sanitation practices and impact behavioral patterns by creating infrastructure in homes, imparting education and empowering a village to increase its capacity to manage water and sanitation resources. Sowmya's success cannot be credited to any single big idea or interventions, but to a series of small steps performed with diligence, good humor, and a relentless focus, which in turn created a sanitation awakening.

"As we clamor aboard a crowded rickshaw we are greeted with the following news: 'There is an outbreak of dengue fever in the village!' It is, however, the last rickshaw of the night. So outbreak or not there is no turning back. We are heading to Rehabilitation Colony #3 (RH3), a small village in rural Karnataka. Originally established to accommodate Bengali refugees in the 1970s, RH3 still has the temporary feel of a refugee camp. But for Sowmya, who spent a year there working on a sanitation project, it also feels like home," recalls Jared Buono after visiting his wife, Sowmya Somnath's project site.

In January 2008, Sowmya, 31, a successful registered engineer with nearly a decade of professional experience left her job and home in the US for a year of grassroots service in rural Karnataka. Sowmya spent the Fellowship year creating sanitation infrastructure in homes and empowering a village to increase its capacity to manage water and sanitation resources. Already well-established as a structural engineer and stocked with an impressive resume of service, Sowmya saw grassroots experience in India as important to her own development.

Sowmya says, "I talk a lot about making use of the tools that you have in hand, not the ones you wish you had. I talk about creating opportunities from problems. I talk about leading a fearless life, a big life, a life of energy and daring. Well, this year was a fantastic exercise in realizing the truth of those statements, and then actually living them."

When Sowmya arrived to RH3 she found a different reality on the ground from the one she had anticipated. Her partner organization, Swami Vivekananda Youth Movement, was 24 hours away in Mysore; the main language spoken was Bengali, not the Tamil she knew or the Kannada she frantically learned; and the team of hygiene educators that she was there to train did not exist. Instead of losing hope to frustration and despite being far out of her comfort zone, Sowmya embraced the situation.

According to 2006 Indicorps Fellow Tanya Sehgal, who was Sowmya's Fellowship support in 2008: "Sowmya worked so hard at language during orientation because she really wanted to hit the ground running. It was so absurd when she got to her project site and realized that Bengali was the language spoken. Really, the whole thing was just a comedy of errors. I wonder though, if I see it that way because Sowmya told it that way. What could have otherwise been an extremely frustrating experience, the kind that makes you want to quit, instead became the kind of experience that made me laugh until tears came out of my eyes because of Sowmya's attitude."

In India, sanitation is not just a problem of infrastructure and resources; it is also one of mind-set. Statistics show that India has more mobile phones than toilets. Sowmya's project to improve sanitation in practice was aimed at addressing issues of open defecation, contaminated drinking water, and un-hygienic habits that are common in parts of India. She specifically focused on creating behavioral change. Dr. Seetharam, SVYM President and surgeon, says, "The project that we were proposing to implement was a relatively new venture. The overall objective was to create an entry into the community and build a rapport with the people and local non-profit organizations, as much as to ensure implementation of the physical targets of the project."

Swami Vivekananda Youth Movement
www.svym.net

The Swami Vivekananda Youth Movement (SVYM) began in 1984 by a group of doctors-to-be in rural Karnataka. The entry through health services helped SVYM to evolve into an organisation working for comprehensive development and empowerment of communities. SVYM operates two hospitals, two learning centers, and a leadership institute in Mysore. SVYM implements over 50 projects ranging from a mobile health outreach program, creation of rural infrastructure, to training, research and advocacy.

A Sanitation Awakening

Drawing from her background as an engineer, Sowmya also oversaw the construction of toilets in RH3, bridging attitudinal change with action.

RH3 consists of around 400 households. The village was formed in 1971, after millions of refugees fled from religious and political violence, from what is now present day Bangladesh. Sanitation is an area of great concern in RH3. A main canal which runs through RH3 provided villagers with water for washing clothes and bathing. Informal surveys suggest that only 30 percent to 40 percent of households in RH3 used latrines. Villagers often used fields, located some distance from their homes, for defecation. The situation was especially difficult for women, who were often forced to wait until dark for privacy.

When Sowmya arrived, she witnessed children defecating in and near their homes, as well as alongside the canal and the water pumps. Villagers were susceptible to waterborne illnesses, such as typhoid and cholera, caused by fecal contamination of drinking water. She also found that diarrhea was rampant.

Sowmya says, "Unlike other development problems in India, you do not need to refer to studies or surveys to understand the sanitation problem. Whether you live in an urban or rural setting, whether you are rich or poor, you need only step outside your dwelling and you can see people defecating and urinating outside, improper disposal of garbage, poor hygiene habits and a general tolerance towards dangerous and easily preventable practices that adversely affect health."

During the year, Sowmya organized street-cleanups, built toilets, and conducted a health and hygiene campaign in schools. In short, sanitation became Sowmya's life. While Sowmya drew from her engineering background for the technical aspects of the project, she also bonded with the families of RH3, making them her own.

Sowmya's willingness to learn and openness to receiving enabled these deeper connections. She says, "There is a humility and wonder that comes with wearing your struggles on your sleeve — humility when you realize it doesn't matter how smart you are if you can't make a human connection, and a wonder when you realize how much people are willing to invest in you even before they have proof that you're a person worth investing in."

The investment was mutual. "Sowmya's presence was — and still is — highly valued by the community. The sheer grit and determination of a total stranger — a woman at that! — staying alone in the village by itself created awe. Sowmya's perseverance despite the resistance she received to some of the concepts she was promoting greatly enhanced the community's respect for her," says Dr. Seetharam.

Being a woman in rural India, and interacting mainly with men was a non-traditional entry into the village. At first, Sowmya's project entailed dealing with exclusively male masons and carpenters; she made special effort to reach out to the women. Sowmya says, "I had to ensure that women could relate to me, as all they had seen was me arguing with the drunken carpenter or reviewing construction techniques with the masons. So I focused on the similarities between myself and them, the fact that I was married, that I cooked, that I ran a household."

Just as Sowmya's relationships in RH3 varied from engineer to neighbor to friend, so did the many activities she devised. Without knowing the language upon arrival, she mimed her way through the Bengali village and quickly captured the hearts of friends and strangers alike. Sowmya engaged school children and teachers with skits, songs, and drawing competitions to promote hand-washing, cleanliness, and the use of garbage cans. She convinced storeowners to install garbage cans outside of their stores. She organized community members to participate in street and canal clean-ups, slowly building a movement in RH3 around hygiene, cleanliness, and sanitation.

Sowmya facilitated the construction of approximately 75 toilets alongside local masons and carpenters. Her role in the process was a multi-faceted one and included verifying material prices, monitoring toilet construction design, checking soil conditions, creating design checklists, educating masons and beneficiaries, and creating stock and contribution records. Throughout, she coordinated with the democratically-elected village council, women's Self Help Groups, and various members of the RH3 community. "Each challenge I encountered created a learning experience or unlocked a tool in myself that I sometimes did not know I had. I learned to wear so many hats," Sowmya remembers.

Prior to Indicorps, Sowmya was a founding member of Watershed Management Group, a non-profit that focuses on community development through natural resource management. Sowmya served as a board member and treasurer for the organization. As a structural engineer for nine years, Sowmya's experiences were diverse. She designed air traffic control towers, performed seismic analyses around the country, and worked on designing one-of-a-kind conveyer belts that crossed national borders. Sowmya served as a Professional Mentor for Engineers without Borders, collaborating with students to

INSPIRE *Sowmya Somnath celebrates a sanitation awakening with a group of school girls after a neighborhood clean-up drive.*

design and construct a community water filtration project in Ghana. She assisted with the resettlement of newly-arrived refugees families in Arizona, building deep connections with Somali families in the process.

With a plethora of challenging professional and service experiences, Sowmya could have felt that she had filled her "quota of service." She could have seen the Indicorps Fellowship as just another challenging situation to add to her story repertoire. Instead, Sowmya made a deep-rooted commitment to RH3 and to the creation of a sanitation awakening.

Since her departure, the culture of sanitation, hygiene, and cleanliness that Sowmya meticulously fostered has blossomed. Slowly, community members have embraced the various behavioral changes which Sowmya advocated. School children regularly wash their hands, often while singing hand-washing songs. Many villagers have stopped burning their garbage. Toilets have also taken on a much larger significance.

Dr. Seetharam, says, "The value of Sowmya's interventions slowly dawned on the community. The awareness about importance of hygiene and sanitation is still a work-in-progress, but from a near-zero state to the current level, there has been significant movement. Sowmya's efforts in generating awareness, has ensured that the people who have built their toilets, value what they have got. The tendency to use the toilet as an additional 'room', so apparent elsewhere, was conspicuously absent in RH3 when one of our teams visited the village nearly a year after Sowmya's work."

Over time, the families of RH3 witnessed the depth of Sowmya's commitment. How she led her life in RH3 reflected the intentionality with which villagers existed on a daily basis. As Sowmya says, "When I talked to Dr. Seetharam about closing out my project, he asked me to make a list — when I put everything down in bullet-points it felt

A Sanitation Awakening

like I had done a lot. What the villagers seemed most impressed with however, was my persistence. A lot of what I was doing was behavior change and doing it in seven months seems non-sensical. However, they recognized my persistence, which is funny because their whole existence is about persistence. They fled their lives in current day Bangladesh and were relocated to a very different community in Karnataka, and then figured out how to make a life for themselves."

Over time, Sowmya fully immersed herself in RH3. One of the strongest relationships she had was with Sudhanya, a local organic farmer and his wife, Shila. Sudhanya had two years of formal schooling and taught himself to read. Through half-broken conversations about topics ranging from the purpose of existence to Sowmya's project, the two formed a relationship that would take on repercussions across the globe. Sudhanya was an active supporter of Sowmya's activities participating in trash clean-ups and learning to lead hygiene workshops. Just as Sudhanya saw Sowmya's passion in her project, Sowmya witnessed his independence of thought and passion for organic farming. Inspired by Sowmya's beliefs in service, Sudhanya followed suit and took his organic farming knowledge to Ethiopia where he didn't know the language or culture.

Sowmya recalls "I was astonished by this move. How would an Indian villager, who didn't know the language or culture, where he would be perceived as an outsider, cope with such a different environment? How would he get anything done? He laughed at me and pointed out how I had been in just that position when I arrived at RH3."

For Sowmya, her Indicorps Fellowship year provided fresh perspective and new resolve. Sowmya says, "I enjoyed the work I was doing prior to coming to India, but I was ready for something new. I didn't want to just do something different, I wanted to do it differently. I think much has been made of all that I did before coming to the Fellowship, but I think it is important to be open and receptive so that your background allows you to see and do more, rather than close you off."

In 2009, after a year apart, Jared joined Sowmya in an epic move from Tucson, Arizona to India to implement community-based water management projects. As Sowmya and Jared build both a life and organization in India committed to sustainable, lasting change, it has been the choices they have made that distinguish their experience. Sowmya and Jared believe the details are important, maintaining a consistent and calculated approach in all they do.

Sowmya says, "It's hard to see the effects of your work when you're in the middle of it, especially when working in something like sanitation. But the link between health and hygiene was reinforced during a health epidemic [in RH3]. Dengue fever hit the village after I had left and a lot of villagers got sick. Those that did not clean up stagnant water near their homes were especially affected. When I came back to visit, the shopkeeper said, 'We got dengue, and we thought of you.' I was momentarily flummoxed to be associated with dengue, but much more enthused when I learned that they conducted trash drives and rallied local government leaders to help clean up the village. The fact that the community took ownership on their own to comprehend and address the epidemic illuminated the often hidden impacts of development."

More than a Destination

Several generations removed from India, Amrit Dhir embarked on the Fellowship in 2008 with Delhi-based non-profit Manzil. While transitioning the organization's leadership from the founder to the next generation, Amrit taught relatively unorthodox English classes with Beatles songs, films on the US Civil Rights Movement, and spontaneous interactions outside the classroom. In return, the Manzil community engaged Amrit in music jams and provocative conversations, motivating him to contemplate alternative perspectives on success. The deeper Amrit explored the magic behind Manzil's incredible learning environment, the more he discovered about himself, and the more effective he became in fostering change.

Sometimes the ordinary is extraordinary. 2008 Indicorps Fellow Amrit Dhir's presence at Manzil is one such instance. Amrit effortlessly submerged into the magic of Manzil's flow: he absorbed the organization's philosophy and simultaneously strengthened Manzil's mission with his own insights and contributions.

Enter Manzil — an enchanting place nestled between the expensive boutiques, bars, and restaurants of Khan Market in New Delhi. Most people who visit Manzil in Flat 13 discover a buzzing activity center, with students engaged in classes, choreographed dance practices, and lively discussions. Quickly, the hustle and bustle of consumerist Delhi disappears as you find yourself absorbed in the profoundness of their mission.

Reminiscent of a new age Peter Pan that embodies an affirmation of free-thinking and limitless possibility, Manzil's Founder Ravi Gulati envisions an alternative to the narrow definitions of success offered by mainstream education. A graduate from IIM-Ahmedabad, one of the top business schools in the world, Gulati bypassed the corporate world to invest in the potential of youth.

Gulati started Manzil in his home as a small intervention to improve math, computer, and English skills for students in nearby quarters. Gulati's aim was to provide an alternative to the status quo of apathy, rote memorization, and mediocrity in government schools. His approach transforms students and volunteers alike in a way that shifts the paradigm of education. "Manzil's journey has been one of constantly discovering the inter-connectedness of all life. It is this thought that infuses our work and vision, and illuminates our understanding of education and empowerment," says Gulati. The alternative that Manzil presents is interactive, vibrant, and ever-changing.

Amrit stepped into this remarkable place from a Masters program at Maastricht University (the Netherlands) to help transition the leadership from Gulati to Manzil's next generation. Although new to the Manzil rhythm, Amrit did not miss a beat. His approach reflected a harmony between his head, heart, and hands, which further strengthened the organization's vision. At Manzil, Amrit found his wings by enabling others to find theirs. The Manzil community seamlessly embraced Amrit into the flow as his openness, ingenuity, and commitment reflected their core philosophy.

In 2008, Amrit set foot in India for the first time, drawn by Indicorps' and Manzil's missions and the seemingly impossible task of transition. For Amrit, born and raised in Los Angeles (California), India remained a distant land that his family left generations earlier for East Africa, and eventually the United States.

"I was the first in at least two generations to come back to live in India," says Amrit. "Before Indicorps, the only impressions of India for me were those that I could borrow from the colors and clichés of newspapers, movies, and books. Indicorps presented an opportunity not just to visit and observe, but also to dig beyond the surface, share, and contribute. Line after line of the Manzil project description emerged as if it had been written for me. The introduction spoke of leadership development and youth empowerment, themes reflecting the work I had done and loved, during my bachelors and beyond. Curiosity and creativity are, for me, two of the most important ingredients for a rich and healthy approach to learning; and Manzil, at its very core, champions these."

Manzil
www.manzil.in

Since 1996, Manzil has touched more than 4000 young people by engaging their critical thinking skills, broadening their educational exposure, and creating opportunities for the exploration of extracurricular and creative talents. An open, welcoming ambiance and thoughtful interactions are essential components of the Manzil experience. At Manzil, teachers are students and students are teachers. Student-led initiatives (such as rock bands and theater) supplement the staple English, computer, and math tutorials.

More Than A Destination

UNITE Amrit Dhir leads a self-designed grammar game with a group of students in Sujan Singh Park. At Manzil, both teaching and learning extend beyond the walls of the traditional classroom to incorporate everyday living.

Amrit thrived in Manzil's proactive learning environment. He quickly immersed himself in the organization's unique culture, which often keeps Flat 13 abuzz long after the shops close, with self-composed music, chess matches, and engaging debates.

While his students echoed the pulse of the capital with the latest ringtones and fashions, Amrit, the towering 6'3" Punjabi with a voracious appetite and an equally captivating enthusiasm, engaged the Manzil youth to question and challenge their preconceptions. He participated in late night music jam sessions, led adventurous outings, and was always willing to stay after class to carry on discussions with his students. Amrit never complained about the long hours, the sparse accommodations, or the drama of teenage interactions. He lived in the Sujan Singh Park quarters adjacent to Khan Market alongside many of his students and their families. Known affectionately as *bhaiya* (elder brother), Amrit became a part of the community, regularly interacting with his students, their parents, and his neighbors.

Manzil dissolves the distinction between the student and the teacher in other ways. The organization's core philosophy is one where every individual possesses certain skills that can be transferred, or taught, to others. Therefore, a teacher in one context may be a student in another.

This paradigm also instills the belief that one can learn through teaching. Reena, 15, a student in an advanced English language class and a teacher in a beginning English language class, holds that "the teacher is the biggest student in the class because the only way to enable someone else to learn, is if you have learned yourself."

Not only does the Manzil structure challenge students to teach others, but it also instills a sense of leadership and responsibility. Vipin, 22, an English language student and guitar teacher feels that "the most challenging and most invigorating part about teaching is being asked a question to which I don't know the answer. I'll tell the student that I don't know but after class when the student begins his homework, I also begin mine."

Amrit's primary project focused on transitioning Manzil's management from its founder to its student leaders in this unique learning environment. For weeks, Amrit wholeheartedly looked, listened, and learned. He studiously observed the ongoing operational practices and elicited feedback from many different Manzil teachers, volunteers, and students. Over time, Amrit assembled a strategy for a new leadership structure, which identified different administrative roles with specific responsibilities, including various Subject Coordinators, a Chief Coordinator, and a team specially dedicated to piloting new initiatives.

Both Amrit and Gulati expected Anish Singh, one of Gulati's first students, a former Manzil teacher, budding thespian, and active member of the Manzil team, to fill the role of Chief Coordinator. In the final month of Amrit's Fellowship, however, Singh received an offer to join a drama troupe in the National School of Drama. This was a dream nurtured at Manzil and an achievement which, while encouraged by Amrit, disrupted the original transition plan.

The systems Amrit put in place, and more importantly the process of assembling a new structure, benefitted Manzil greatly. Although a complete transition to a student-led administration could not be fully achieved, the outcome was fruitful. "When I came to Manzil, Anish was set to be the point person for just about everything. By decentralizing duties and creating a multi-tiered system, we strengthened the leadership base and eased the burden of responsibility from one person to many."

Furthermore, as Amrit explains, the process itself was empowering: "In a first for Manzil, we held a formal written application and interview process for an administrative position, thus building practical skills while fostering ownership and making leadership accessible to all."

Exposure to a professional selection process provided the Manzil students an opportunity to reflect on their leadership potential and articulate their own individual qualities.

While Amrit's main project was to assist in a leadership transition for Manzil, it was his role as mentor, teacher, friend, and neighbor for which the community most remembers him. Amrit reinforced Manzil's core educational processes. As an English teacher, Amrit infused aspects of history, geography, and "much-needed" general knowledge.

Amrit converted the entirety of Khan Market, and the rich cultural opportunities in the surrounding vicinity, into a playground of learning. In order to improve his students' English and build their self-confidence, Amrit created prompts that required them to venture out into Khan Market and converse with foreigners, which at first intimidated many students, but eventually became a class favorite. In addition to providing real-world experience and exposure to diverse populations, such activities extended the classroom onto the streets they traversed daily and built confidence. By merging the classroom with everyday life, students had practical opportunities to apply the "Manzil philosophy."

Additionally, Amrit took his students to film screenings, lecture series, and plays at various cultural centers. A film series at the Indian Habitat Center on the U.S. Civil Rights Movement was particularly eye-opening. Amrit says, "We used those films to discuss topics of inequality and discrimination. Students were exposed to an unfamiliar U.S. history, and were able to draw parallels to both historical and present-day issues in India." Amrit made the human experience in foreign places relevant to his students in a way that added texture to the leadership Manzil was instilling. He was able to paint a picture that revealed how community change can start with the individual.

Amrit drew from his own passions and life experiences to encompass non-traditional media of education in basic subjects like English. In multiple classes, he employed his personal collection of rock music as a central aid. One of the students' favorites (and a song many of them are proud to sing a year later) is The Beatles' song *In My Life*. "There is so much depth to that song," Amrit explains. "So many layers and a complexity accessed through a remarkably simple vocabulary. It was almost like a literature class. Teaching through lyrics is much more interesting than teaching through grammar."

Even when Amrit faced situations that were culturally different, he sought to understand without judgment. "I was careful not to jump to conclusions and conscientious in not being unnecessarily vocal or critical. As my friends at Manzil got to know me and understand me, they could ascertain my protests without my having to say anything. At that point, it was the group questioning and debating and thinking. And, when I was included in the conversation, it was not as that outsider, but as one of the group; a fellow contributor and learner."

Amrit embraced Manzil's philosophy of creative learning and principled living. Gulati says, "Amrit rooted himself in an honest community. He developed confidence, relationships, and family. He became a role model and brought energy, motivation, and a sense of equality. Nothing spectacular happened, and that is a reflection of his complete immersion. That in itself is noteworthy. Amrit's big achievement was coming from a different journey and still finding a way to contribute wholly. He totally became a part of the stream without losing his individuality."

Amrit's personal learning seemed only fitting at a place like Manzil where, as Gulati frames it, "We are all learners here. And like life itself, any *manzil* (destination) is only a sojourn." As Amrit deliberates on issues of justice and fairness in law school and beyond, the Manzil outlook will continue to shape his journey and impact the choices he makes. "While I wouldn't say I have ever really accepted the mainstream anyway, Manzil and Indicorps let me live an alternative that was so far outside the realm of what I previously even considered possible. Put simply, it has changed me."

8

The Eternal Voice

In 2009, Fellow Pooja Shahani traveled from Hong Kong to establish community radio at Shramik Bharti in Kanpur, Uttar Pradesh. Pooja's year in the villages displayed what is possible in a seemingly short span of time. She created community radio infrastructure and helped assemble a team of volunteer reporters who in turn produced and narrow-casted high quality radio programs. The radio programs then prompted thought-provoking conversations and served as a call to action on gender norms, the importance of sanitation, and the debilitating nature of addictive substances. Pooja's dedicated efforts to giving the community a voice led the villagers to believe in themselves and find their own solutions.

People slowly trickled into Chunni Chachi's courtyard in the village of Anoopur. By noon, a crowd of nearly 30 villagers — mostly girls and women — settled down in the shade to listen to the *Waqt Ki Awaaz* (The Eternal Voice) narrow-cast. Over the next hour, the crowd listened to the pre-recorded radio programs, featuring voices from their own village.

At twenty-minute intervals, between gratifying breezes of wind, the audience discusses whether their daughters should be allowed out, what clothes they should wear, and who is to blame in cases of sexual abuse. As the loudspeakers transmit familiar — and at times, familial — voices, the girls, normally reserved, beam with pride. In one short year, 2009 Indicorps Fellow Pooja Shahani has brought the voices of villagers into the homes of a much broader community.

What is possible in a year? Development experts, Indicorps alumni, and experienced field workers alike will generally tell you nothing happens in a year when it comes to making societal change. Traditions and practices become cemented over thousands of years; changing them in one year is unlikely at best. Yet, Pooja's Fellowship year is an example of the change that can be inspired in a matter of months. Partnered with Kanpur-based non-profit Shramik Bharti, Pooja played an integral role in the development of a community radio program (*Waqt ki Awaaz*) that is generating waves in Kanpur and its surrounding villages. Today, local Kanpur radio stations are broadcasting *Waqt ki Awaaz* programs to an expansive audience; the Shramik Bharti team continues to narrow-cast the same programs in villages lacking electricity.

Broadcasts play programs over radio airwaves, while narrow-casts play recorded programs over speakers to a live audience. Narrow-casting provides a unique opportunity to build community through group listening sessions that are followed by discussions. The community radio team goes out into the village and calls as many people as they can to listen. Each narrow-cast hour includes dramas, comedies, and folk songs. Each program speaks to a different social issue — addiction to *paan masala*, open-defecation, the importance of girls' education, and more.

Pooja's arrival in Kanpur marked the commencement of Shramik Bharti's foray into radio. Rakesh Pandey, Senior Manager of Programs, proudly says, "Producing radio programs is an artisanry. I always wanted to use radio in our ongoing community efforts. And then I thought of Indicorps. Pooja's arrival established community radio in Shramik Bharti."

Under the lead of Radha Shukla, a 15-year Shramik Bharti veteran, a powerful community mobilizer, and an amazingly strong woman, Pooja quickly became the passionate advocate behind the project. Together, Pooja and Shukla assembled a volunteer team of field reporters, produced nine programs with eleven more in the pipeline, and captured a weekly slot on Gyaanvani radio, a local Kanpur station.

Pandey's vision for the community radio project was to create programming that inspired communities to think about what they heard and translate that thinking into action. "Radio stations should

Shramik Bharti
www.shramikbharti.org.in

Shramik Bharti, which literally means "empowering the laborer", has strong trade union roots. Founded in 1986, Shramik Bharti focuses on poverty alleviation and community building. Shramik Bharti has utilized the women's Self Help Group (SHG) model to improve lives and create opportunities for people residing in the slums of and rural villages around Kanpur. Projects include: sustainable agriculture, water, sanitation, livelihoods, and health initiatives for both rural and urban communities. In 2009, Shramik Bharti launched a community radio initiative to share information and connect its various efforts.

CONNECT Pooja Shahani often focused on getting to know the girls of the village to encourage them to recognize the importance of their voice.

IGNITE Women participate at a narrow-casting in the village of Hindupur where they contemplate a radio drama on the importance of sanitation.

be able to not only raise awareness but motivate people to take action. Community radio has tremendous scope provided there is community ownership," says Pandey. The community directly decides what they want to hear by creating the programming themselves. *Waqt ki Awaaz* programs so far have addressed issues of girls' education, safe drinking water, sanitation, anemia, and reproductive health.

"[Our goal is] to break the culture of silence. We want to challenge viewpoints and show the other side. We create a lot of boundaries when we are comfortable, so our goal is to make people uncomfortable," says Pandey. By cultivating discussion on unspoken topics, Pandey hopes that communities will be able to bridge the gaps that impede India's progress. The newly-sparked dialogue complements Shramik Bharti's 20 years of community involvement through Self-Help Groups, health interventions, and livelihood support.

With Shramik Bharti's guidance, Pooja ventured out into villages surrounding Kanpur. The community radio project began with Pooja and Shukla organizing community meetings in twelve villages in the Maihta block of Kanpur Dehat, where Shramik Bharti had already built a strong reputation. Pooja and Shukla explained the idea of community radio, how it could be used as a tool for social transformation, and the importance of community involvement through field reporting, scriptwriting, and music. In the first several months, Pooja, Shukla and a team of seven volunteer reporters set out discussing various issues with villagers, writing and re-writing scripts, and painstakingly editing their programs.

In January 2010, *Waqt ki Awaaz* narrow-casted its first program on respect for the elderly. The program featured a story of a woman who locks her aging father-in-law in a room without food, two short interviews with elderly villagers relaying their personal experiences, and a song highlighting the need for inter-generational harmony. The program prompted a powerful, emotional response from the community. Several audience members openly wept.

Pooja remembers, "It was really encouraging to see people's reactions, because we didn't know we could get this type of response. I have watched as our listeners react to the radio program. They laugh when it's funny, they cry when it's sad, they curse when they dislike the characters and they sing to their folk songs. We're reaching their hearts. Now, we have to slowly bring that energy to their hands and legs so they can transform their emotions into actions."

The *Waqt ki Awaaz* programs have impacted the villages where the team is narrow-casting. A program on the value of toilets evoked an immediate response in the village of Hindupur: five families, who had converted their outhouses into storage, re-instated their intended use. Another woman without a toilet took the initiative to build one. Several girls dug the pits necessary to install them. Groups of people took oaths to quit eating *paan masala* after hearing a program dedicated to its harmfulness. When the same program was broadcast on the radio, families called in and shared their own experiences with addiction. In Anoopur, several teenage girls who knew Pooja as a radio-*wali* came up and asked if they could produce their own song and perform their own drama for a future program.

Since that first narrow-cast in January 2010, *Waqt ki Awaaz* has maintained a steady presence in the twelve villages of Maihta block and drawing an audience has become easier: many people readily attend and are excited about hearing new programs. According to Pooja, "[Narrow-casting] is a place where you can bring a whole community together. It's a collective gathering where people are engaged and can talk openly. It's a space where women and girls can talk about everything. Your questions are answered immediately. There's a lot of thought process involved in narrow-casting that is lost in broadcasting."

The impact has not been limited to the airwaves and villages. The *Waqt ki Awaaz* team encompasses diversity in gender, caste, educational levels, and religion. It consists of talented song-writers, musical directors, and radio personalities. Pooja says, "I've seen them take more ownership over reporting, recording, and scriptwriting. They are willing to stand up and talk, even in front of strangers. They are much more confident. The Muslim-Hindu dynamic has evolved as well. They eat at each other's houses. They don't think about religion anymore, they just look at each other as people."

Team members credit their involvement in the radio project for personal and professional development. In addition to developing powerful communication and media skills, *Waqt ki Awaaz* has prompted them to understand the power of their own voices. Liyaqat, an 18-year old volunteer says, "Before I used to use a lot of foul language when I spoke. Now, I'm more respectful in the way I speak. Everyone says that I've changed. They like listening to me speak. If I can change myself, I can change my community."

The impact on Pooja has been equally robust. "I lived in India for two years when I was a teenager. The biggest change I see in myself is my mindset. The lifestyle I choose to live now comes with a constant attention to every decision I make and how it affects people around me."

During her Fellowship year, Pooja joined two other 2009 Indicorps fellows in experimenting with Gandhi's eleven vows. The vow that spoke most to Pooja was *satya* (truth). "What I learned most when following my vow of honesty was that more than being honest with others, you have to be honest with yourself. I think many times we run away from our truths by focusing on our external environment. I took the courage to raise fundamental concerns, but made sure what I said and did wasn't hurting anyone. I wanted my honesty to lift others, not to destroy another's confidence."

In April 2010, local Kanpur radio station Gyanvani 106.4 FM agreed to air *Waqt ki Awaaz* programs over airwaves that reach an 80 kilometer radius. *Waqt ki Awaaz* now has regular slots every Monday at 9:30 am and 5:30 pm. Gyanvani's regular broadcast provided the first big breakthrough for the team. Since then, Pooja and Shukla have connected with IIT-Kanpur, one of India's most prestigious universities, which has expressed an interest in airing *Waqt ki Awaaz* programs from their own campus radio station. While Pooja and Shukla have assembled a dedicated team, developed quality programs, created a name for Waqt ki Awaaz through narrow-casting and aired on local radio stations, the process has not been without difficulty.

Pooja's Fellowship year was characterized by the ups and downs that come with intense grassroots service. Initially scheduled to be a part of an Indicorps team of four at Shramik Bharti, Pooja was the only Fellow who ended up there, as the others withdrew before the Fellowship started. Further, Pooja notes, "I didn't know anything about community radio and neither did they (Shramik Bharti)." Editing sound clips was very time intensive and required great attention to detail. "We spent days listening to hours and hours of recorded material. Deciding upon which clips to use and not use was tough. Sometimes we listened to 50 clips and only used two."

Breaking ground through a new medium and overcoming both internal and external skepticism added difficulty to the already challenging process. A small, volunteer-dependent team limits the immediate reach and creates opportunities for conflict. Since several volunteers are from the same village, when tensions arise, they often fester at home and become a family affair. Another pressing challenge is a lack of funding to sustain the project. Pandey estimates a cost of $500,000 to operate Shramik Bharti's own radio station. Despite a number of unsuccessful grant applications, Pandey remains hopeful: "We don't get any rejections, we just get regrets. I know someday it will happen."

The potential of *Waqt ki Awaaz* is the potential of people's voices to shape their future and our collective consciousness. Pooja says,

"Empowerment means having a voice and giving a space to people to fully express themselves." For every individual there is a story. In every voice heard, greater freedom echoes.

What is possible in one year? How do you measure the impact of 525,600 minutes? In radio broadcasts, village meetings, or lives touched? The *Waqt Ki Awaaz* project is a testament to what is possible in a handful of months, with a few volunteers, and a shoestring budget. Yet, the visible and prominent successes of the *Waqt Ki Awaaz* project and Pooja's efforts are only part of the story — a story whose real success is that it will continue to be told; it will continue to both shape and be shaped by the characters in it; and it will, like the radio waves, ripple into the hearts and minds of countless others.

Innovations
in Social Change

Launched in 2006, the Grassroots Development Laboratory (GDL) combined the Piramal Foundation's penchance for social business with Indicorps' model of intensive community immersion and personal growth. Through the four-year experiment ten Indicorps Fellows and numerous short and long-term volunteers engaged in an experiment to find solutions in building local leadership, rural employment, and technology. In the process, GDL yielded four successful social enterprise concepts: Bagar Employment Institute, Mobile Naukri, Source for Change and Sarvajal. GDL also generated deeper insights on how to prompt communities and individuals to think larger than themselves and to create change from within.

The large mandate in the small town of Bagar, Rajasthan, was to find solutions to India's most pressing development challenges. Initiated in 2006, the Grassroots Development Laboratory (GDL) was a real-world "laboratory" that sought to harness the creativity and energy of young people to innovate through entrepreneurship. A partnership between the Piramal Foundation and Indicorps, GDL encouraged on-the-ground experimentation to address major social challenges, including employment and migration, safe drinking water, and women's empowerment.

Anand Shah, CEO of the Piramal Foundation and co-founder of Indicorps, says, "GDL is an experiment to show that young people with real motivation and commitment can solve social problems that have plagued us for decades." The approach was to experiment locally, take what succeeded on the ground in Bagar, look for scaleable processes, and apply them across the country as sustainable practices in India's continuing development. As a laboratory, GDL focused on combining various ideas and strengthening "proof of concept." The business metric to be applied, however, went beyond a mere financial return on investment. The goal was to understand the interdependency of the community as stakeholders and find sustainable, balanced solutions that valued all.

The byproduct of this process has been four successful social enterprise concepts:

Bagar Employment Institute (2006-10)
A finishing school that tackled rural unemployment by providing soft skills training.

Mobile Naukri (2009)
A rural employment initiative that utilizes ever-popular mobile phones to stem migration by linking local employers with local job-seekers.

Source for Change (2007)

An all-women's business process outsourcing (BPO) unit challenging mainstream business assumptions and traditional gender roles in a conservative rural community.

Sarvajal (2007)

A clean drinking water initiative, which combats the public health problem of rampant water-borne illnesses.

Ten Indicorps Fellows and numerous short- and long-term volunteers have infused GDL with energy, creativity, and spirited innovation. In 2010, the GDL experiment evolved from an in-house laboratory into the two-year Piramal Fellowship program placing young business talent with start-up social enterprises throughout India.

Spirited Beginnings

In September 2006, the first batch of Indicorps Fellows arrived in Bagar. Preeti Balakrishnan, Radhika Batra, and Ashish Gupta each embarked on a two-year commitment at GDL under the direction of Anand Shah and Indicorps Staff Member Lakshmi Iyer. The intensive community-building activities in the first two years laid a strong foundation for GDL's subsequently successful ventures. Indicorps' first year in Bagar focused on community immersion. This included neighborhood

Grassroots Development Laboratory
www.piramal.org

The Grassroots Development Laboratory ("GDL") was a joint initiative in 2006 by Indicorps and the then newly-established Ajay G. Piramal Foundation in the ancestral town of the Piramal family: Bagar, Rajasthan. The Piramal Foundation is a private philanthropic foundation that is in search of scaleable solutions to India's most pressing challenges. As a four-year experiment, GDL focused on empowering women, providing clean drinking water, building leadership capacity, as well as encouraging local employment and rural entrepreneurship.

clean-ups, cricket matches, health awareness campaigns, informal tutoring sessions, and an unwavering presence in the kitchens and courtyards of Bagar. These short-term experiments created a base in the community and a greater understanding of the community's needs and aspirations. Radhika remembers, "I was surprised to learn that

EMPOWER *Local women are the drivers of the business and development processes at Source for Change in this otherwise conservative community.*

nearly 40 percent of the male population migrated for jobs to places like Mumbai and the Middle East. With a flow of remittances, Bagar did not seem like an impoverished place, and yet there was still so much to do."

With ever-developing community empathy, Radhika rallied women's self-help groups. Preeti organized leadership camps with local school children. Ashish experimented with basic computer and English classes. Each of the small-scale interventions bought tremendous goodwill. The energy that Preeti, Radhika, and Ashish invested those first two years paid huge dividends over GDL's tenure.

The process was not without false starts, personal setbacks, and at times, collective disarray. Fellows struggled with finding their roles, sustaining projects beyond their individual interests, and engaging the community to genuinely care about its collective future. At one point, Ashish's dream of creating a rural technological revolution sputtered into simple computer classes for a handful of youth. However, these humble beginnings eventually led to GDL's multiple social enterprise concepts, including the Bagar Employment Institute (BEI).

Meaningful Aspirations

GDL's most consistent experiments have addressed the ongoing problem of unemployment. Bagar is known as a local education hub. With approximately 35 schools and colleges in the area, 90 percent of the population under age thirty has at least an 8th grade education and many hold bachelors or masters degrees. Despite the high level of formal education, the challenge of finding employment is an issue in Bagar, and indeed remains one in towns and villages across India.

The Bagar Employment Institute (BEI) hoped to catalyze new excitement around career prospects and purposeful living. BEI began in 2007 with a room full of computers, a few students who spent the day at GDL, and a homemade curriculum based on intense personal coaching. The key was to show the students that education was not

IMMERSE Radhika Batra's early efforts in organizing a women's self-help group in Bagar was followed by four successful GDL start-ups including women-led Source for Change.

simply about learning technical skills, but about the approach and the excitement of challenging oneself. Kaushal Rajoriya, BEI Managing Director says, "Ashish saw that people had education and talent but needed the platform to make their education more practical. He built strong community relations and invested wholly in developing each student's mind and heart." Everyone in Bagar fondly remembers Ashish as a brother, son, or friend who dedicated two years to creating something positive and lasting in that corner of rural Rajasthan.

To date, 25 batches and over 300 students have passed through BEI. Rajoriya says, "The benefit of BEI is that local people not only learned skills, but learned how the market changes, and how to be comfortable, motivated, and self-driven." Over the years BEI has refined its curriculum based on feedback from its students who have received jobs in Jaipur and the nearby towns of Jhunjhunu and Sikar. 2008 Indicorps Fellow Pulkit Agrawal further innovated on the BEI curriculum by introducing an entrepreneurship development program and business consultancy for small rural enterprises.

The energy that went into creating BEI is visible years later in the students who fill the various classrooms to become teachers, retail salespeople, IT technicians, and legal clerks. The Indicorps' effect echoes in the students' aspirations and eagerness to set goals, seek meaningful employment, and excel.

With GDL's evolution, the BEI chapter will end. However, over its three-year existence, BEI injected a level of meaningful aspiration into the local youth population. "The BEI experiment showcased one way that the standard of technology education in rural areas could be raised enough that youth in the community could see, and come to believe, that technology and tech skills are not just an urban privilege. Rural youth, too, can perform," says Ashish.

Technology for Jobs

As an outgrowth of BEI and the realization that most of the jobs available to educated youth required migration to big cities, 2009 Indicorps Fellows Sahil Chaudry and Vivake Prasad initiated Mobile Naukri to connect local youth to local jobs. What is unique about Mobile Naukri is that it promotes a rural-rural solution rather than a rural-urban or urban-rural one.

Still in the nascent stage, Mobile Naukri is a BEI spin-off business service which uses SMS messaging to alert youth about local job opportunities in their education bracket. At the beginning, Sahil hunted down promising opportunities at local companies. Vivake interviewed qualified youth at the BEI training center. In the first six months, Sahil and Vivake contacted over 100 employers and created a database of 1,500 qualified youth jobseekers. In May 2010, Mobile Naukri sent out an SMS to its first batch of interviewees for a packager position at biscuit company Parle-G's local factory.

Sahil explains, "Mobile Naukri provided a bridge for people who did not have access to growth opportunities in their hometown. We hoped that by strengthening local businesses with quality employees in the local area, we could address local unemployment, and stem labor migration." Mobile Naukri aimed to transform the region by developing a more connected, stimulated rural economy. With over 700,000 villages and small towns languishing in the contemporary urban-centric economy, the potential of invigorating rural India by a simple re-ordering of human capital is pioneering.

As with any start-up, Sahil and Vivake tackled all aspects of business operations and wore many hats. Sahil reflects, "I believe that we were able to learn quickly because we had love for the people we were working for and faith that no matter the temporary setbacks, we could make the dream of Mobile Naukri a reality. On a personal level, I have learned that struggle is the way the universe pushes us to grow. When I feel challenged, I know that the universe is pushing me to grow and that the answer to overcoming my challenge and feeling happy is hidden in the questions that arise from my struggle."

The future of Mobile Naukri will depend in large part on how the organization can adapt to tackle the operational and technological demands that appear as usage grows. Even so, the experiment of adopting a fairly universal technology to add efficiencies to the crucial, and increasingly faltering, process of local employment is significant. Mobile Naukri showed that both a positive impact on local quality of life as well as a curbing of the rate of urban migration is possible with grassroots tools and smart design.

A Different Spin on Local Employment

In 2007, GDL launched Source for Change, an all-women's rural business process outsourcing company (BPO) that handles data-entry, Hindi-based voice services, and web-research on a contract basis for companies and institutions around the world. Women joining a technologically-savvy enterprise in the Shekawat region of Rajasthan is a trail-blazing notion — especially considering that the community still observes the *pardah* system (in which women veil their faces in the presence of men).

Operating from a center in Bagar, Source for Change trains local women to be proficient in various computer applications. Saroj Yogi, a 25 year-old employee of Source for Change from the nearby village of Bhaktawarpura, says, "In the first two months we learned Excel, Word and other [Microsoft] Office applications. Today it is an electronic age and it is useful to learn [these skills]. Before I used to do just housework, now I work [at Source for Change] for eight hours a day. I have moved from fear to confidence."

Although both males, 2007 Indicorps Fellow Gagan Rana and GDL volunteer Alim Haji recognized that training and employing women would provide a stable workforce and an opportunity for greater gender parity. In the GDL spirit, Gagan and Alim began by making home-to-home personal visits to explain the concept behind their venture. Men in the community were skeptical. They did not believe that their women could operate computers, let alone hold down a steady, skilled job.

On October 4, 2007, Gagan and Alim commenced a six-week training for the first eleven women participants. The women ranged from 18 to 35 and came from a variety of castes. The trainings focused on basic computer and English skills. Since the first training three years ago, Source for Change's impact has gone far beyond the workplace. 2009 Indicorps Fellow Aditi Poddar, who focused on developing women's organizational leadership potential, adds "Seeing how the women have changed is inspiring; they definitely feel more ownership over Source for Change. It used to be just a job for them, but now if something is broken, they take the responsibility to fix it. They don't feel any hesitation in taking the lead on something at home either."

Shrot Katewa, who was born and educated in Mumbai, returned to his ancestral village near Bagar to become the Chief Operations Officer for Source for Change. He recollects, "The first few meetings we had with the clients, we struggled to convince them that rural women were at par, if not better, than any of their urban competitors. After completing the first project, the women of SFC proved more than we could imagine. I knew that SFC could make a big social impact as by the outcome of its vision, we could furnish the exact demands and the needs of the community. I also realized that not only did SFC make social sense by empowering the women in rural areas but also had the potential of being an iconic idea which by replicating throughout rural India, could act as the epicenter of the wave of development of rural India."

Source for Change has conducted several more trainings, employed dozens of additional women, and fielded hundreds of requests from men to employ their wives and daughters. Moreover, today when children in Bagar have technological questions, they run to their mothers before their fathers. While Source for Change has certainly made waves in Bagar, the business model has had ripple effects in other states. Karthik Raman, Indicorps alumnus and Head of Business Development for Source for Change says, "Once a week people call from places like Uttarakhand, Orissa and Tamil Nadu and ask us for our story, how we started, and advice on starting their own rural BPO." In 2010, Source for Change has committed to breaking even and managing operations on its own terms.

Water for All

Connecting Ashish's dream for a technological revolution, GDL's persistent efforts on employment, and an acknowledgement of the harmful effect of fluorosis in the drinking water, Anand Shah and GDL volunteer Naman Shah launched Sarvajal (literally "water for all"). With the positive intent of a public health initiative, Sarvajal aimed to provide safe drinking water at an affordable price. By heavily involving the local population in the water sales, delivery, and franchise management, the for-profit social enterprise also built community ownership of the product and the process.

Anand Shah says, "We've designed a model that requires us to engage with the village, not just install a machine. The model motivates each franchisee to earn a living by becoming a long-term ambassador for better health for his/her neighbors. The bottom line — we fail if people aren't drinking clean water."

The GDL-Indicorps team grew Sarvajal's base the old fashioned way — through grassroots engagement. The Sarvajal team began with door-to-door visits in Bagar and surrounding villages. On the first day of this campaign, they reached 100 families. At first, some people did not see the point of paying for water. Cognizant of the debilitating effect of excess fluoride in water, Uday Singh Chawara, principal at a local primary school in Bagar says, "I started drinking Sarvajal because it had no fluoride. Now my entire family drinks Sarvajal. Even when we go out of town, we take this water with us."

In 2008, Indicorps Fellows Tushar Kansal and Rahul Suresh joined the Sarvajal team and helped it grow from three to thirty franchisees. Tushar devoted his time to managing one of the main franchises near Bagar, personally delivering water to villages, creating a training program for franchisees, and building awareness about water conservation and sanitation through *jal melas* (water festivals). Rahul took up the marketing end, traveling from village to village motivating locals to become customers.

Tushar remembers, "I started thinking about the importance of reaching out to village-dwellers in a country in which seventy percent of the population lives in rural areas... I set up shop in Ashok Nagar [a small village near Bagar] with twenty liters of Sarvajal, a kilo of lemons, and a jar of sugar." From this lemonade stand, Tushar developed relationships with the children of the village, and eventually their parents. He reached out to locals with creative ideas and motivated them to become local distributors. "I asked Miraji, a mother of six children with ineffable strength and grace if she would be a local distributor... I piloted [a model] in another village where a local entrepreneur would deliver twenty-liter bottles of water to his neighbors on his bicycle from a five hundred-liter tank of Sarvajal water we installed in his home."

While franchises are steadily increasing, there are issues related to the amount of waste-water created through reverse-osmosis purification. There are also the continuous challenges of managing the various outlets, marketing the business, and clamping down on franchises that are not always honest in their practices. Sarvajal has created innovative technology solutions for overall quality control, and self-monitoring of the reverse-osmosis machinery's output and maintenance.

As of May 2010, Sarvajal had expanded to 121 rural franchises in Rajasthan, Gujarat, and Maharashtra. In 2009 alone, the company processed 30 million liters of water for over 60,000 people. By 2013, Sarvajal plans to extend to 3,000 villages nationwide. However, the scalability of businesses like Sarvajal is not just limited to water. The belief is that that there can be market-based solutions to meet other basic needs and facilitate social progress. Anand Shah says, "Eventually you hope these social enterprises will be exemplars that give the government answers on how to provide basic services. Or these enterprises will go the way of [the Indian] telecommunications industry, which has provided low cost solutions to people where they need them."

Greater Consciousness

The development sector may ask after four years of GDL operations, "Has GDL succeeded in achieving its goals? Did GDL resolve any of India's most pressing development challenges? Did GDL have any real impact?" GDL's approach to business and social change had far reach in terms of its breadth and the people it involved. All of its initiatives provided livelihood options and hope of what else was possible. Moreover, since GDL was a designated "grassroots development laboratory," the metric for measuring success was not based solely on its outputs, but on whether real experimentation had transpired. A 100% success rate could have simply been a failure in not setting the bar high enough, especially where an ambitious mandate existed.

According to business management professor Prithwiraj Ghorpade who has followed Indicorps' progress and visited GDL in summer 2010: "Ultimately, a laboratory creates the environment for truly meaningful experiments to be conducted such that *all* participants grow in insight, character and competence, irrespective of the specific results of each experiment. The real significance of the Bagar story was that GDL and Indicorps were able to demonstrate with clarity, commitment and sensitivity, that such a laboratory could be attempted even in the real world setting of a rural community with results that probably will go well beyond the ambit of the present and effects that apparently stretch far deeper than the measureable."

GDL's very existence is designed to shift the paradigm on everything — from who to involve, to how you view social problems, to how you measure success. If GDL encouraged greater consciousness on any of these frontiers among the various stakeholders, including the Indicorps Fellows involved, the long-term return on investment will indeed be a sum greater than the total of its parts.

CHAPTER 10

Service for the Soul

Based at the foothills of the Himalayas, August 2008 Fellow Gaurav Madan partnered with democratically-elected village councils and local grassroots organization Chirag to tackle public health challenges. As a rural community organizer, Gaurav led communities to advocate their rights and demand accountability but consistently questioned the value of his efforts and grew restless with the slow pace of change. However, upon his return to Chirag in May 2010, as the narrative lead of Journeys in Service, Gaurav came to understand the lasting impact of patience and the organic nature of community-centered development.

Simayal, a village at the foothills of the Himalayas, was one of the last project sites I visited in preparation for this retrospective on a decade of Indicorps Fellowships. My mission was to evaluate the Indicorps Fellowship program by capturing stories from each of the past ten Fellowship classes and reflecting on the Indicorps philosophy and experience. From Uttarakhand to Karnataka, the Indicorps approach came to life as I tracked the continuing impact from our collective experiments in social change. In city slums and tribal villages, I saw echoes of the Himalayan villages I used to traverse daily. At each partner organization, I was reminded of my own Fellowship project. In each Fellow's story, I saw a part of my own.

I began this journey full of questions about development, social service, and how to bring about social change. I knew that my Fellowship had invigorated my commitment to social justice, but what did it take to make a lasting impact? What mattered years later? Did local communities take ownership? If so, what sustained that ownership?

Reminiscent of my Fellowship year, this five-month journey across the subcontinent allowed me to once more engage with both India and social change, and to explore the transformative nature of intense service. It meant once again living my values in challenging settings. From sleeping on the floors of trains to battling 115-degree temperatures to withstanding indifference and cynicism, the road was bumpy. By that road, I made my way through the winding hills of Uttarakhand, back to my project site and former home in Simayal.

In May 2010, after ten months away I returned to Simayal, where I had been a 2008 Indicorps Fellow. Returning to Chirag (Central Himalayan Rural Action Group), my field partner organization, was an insightful homecoming. I was able to see my Indicorps Fellowship year — the journey, efforts, and struggles — from a fresh perspective. I grasped the significance of both the energy I gave and the frustration I had left behind. It was a profound experience to complete a full circle, while still finding it enriching and new.

My project at Chirag had been: to facilitate the creation of health committees via democratically-elected village councils (*Gram Panchayats*) and build the capacity of these committees to positively impact public health in their villages. The project was a convergence of public health and village governance. Over my Fellowship year, the health committees, Chirag staff, and I had organized health camps for women, demanded children's Vitamin A promised by the district government, and created a venue to address health needs at the most grassroots level.

My Fellowship year had undoubtedly been a valuable one. However, my first six months at Chirag was also characterized by a tremendous amount of frustration and resistance. I put an immense amount of pressure on myself and held everything I did to the highest standard. I struggled with understanding what progress, social change, and development actually looked like on the ground. While I was fully committed to my project, the absence of any results in those first months — or my inability to see how results manifest over time — had

Central Himalayan Rural Action Group (Chirag)
www.chirag.org

Established in 1987, Chirag (Central Himalayan Rural Action Group) is a catalyst for dignity, justice and solidarity in the extremely mountainous and remote Central Himalayas of India. Chirag operates in nearly 250 villages in five districts of the Kumaon region of Uttarakhand with a predominantly local staff. As part of Chirag's rural development interventions, Chirag's field-workers walk from village to village to mobilize communities, to empower women's Self-Help Groups, to re-forest hillsides, and to strengthen village councils.

brought intense feelings of frustration, helplessness, and isolation. I was looking for something immediate and sweeping in a place where gradual change signifies something sustainable and ultimately stronger.

VK Madhavan, Executive Director of Chirag, explained, "It can be slow and painful to try and empower others, but it is well worth it. Today *Gram Pradhans* (council leaders) are going to the PHC (Primary Health Center), they are organizing government health camps, and they are able to demand services that are guaranteed."

While my vision of a complete revolution of the public health system was not realized during my Fellowship year, we nonetheless empowered communities that have since continued to advocate for better access to improved health facilities, initiate activities on their own accord, and raise awareness in villages about public health.

INVEST Gaurav Madan assists in a training of ASHA health workers. Strengthening the capacity of existing government structures remains an important part of Chirag's preventive health approach.

The day I returned, Chirag threw me right back into the field. Over the following week, I walked twelve kilometers a day, participated in health committee meetings in several villages, and provided feedback on the progress I had seen since I left. It was an incredible feeling to reconnect with the people, places, and purpose that defined the most enriching year of my life. It was particularly gratifying to see that our collective efforts had gained further steam.

As a 2008 Indicorps Fellow, my role at Chirag had focused on forming, training, and rallying health committees and other village-based institutions in twelve villages. Upon my return, I happily discovered that progress had been sustained and even expanded since my departure. Since I left, the Baret health committee coordinated with the local government and held a women's health camp; the Kherda health committee organized hemoglobin testing for pregnant women; the Chatola health committee successfully organized a day of *shramdaan* (gift of labor) to clean village water tanks and springs to prevent waterborne illnesses. Almost every health committee continued to monitor drinking water for potability. In Hartola, the health committee had successfully motivated six families to start boiling their water. In Simayal and Killor, the health committees started building *kurra* (trash) pits, something that was never discussed during my time at Chirag.

What was even more exciting was the discovery that health committee members had become enthusiastically aware of their roles, their responsibilities, and the potential of their actions. "People in villages are becoming sensitized to health issues. Supplies are now reaching sub-centers where previously they were not. My vision is that health committees will become strong enough to be able to fully assess the health condition and act upon it," said Lata Harbola, Preventive Health Program Coordinator at Chirag.

Alongside women like Harbola, I helped to introduce year-long health action plans in multiple areas. Since I left, 40 health committees have

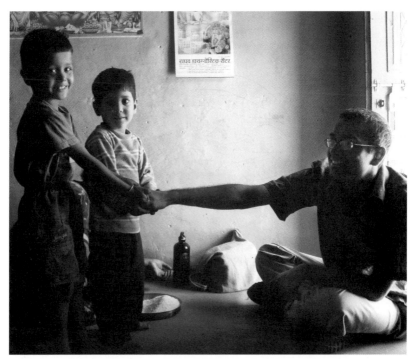

REACH Gaurav Madan catches up with a family in Simayal. Making house visits and establishing relationships with community members was an integral part of building a community-based movement around health.

REFLECT The rugged Himalayan terrain meant re-examining community organizing, development and social change from a nuanced perspective rooted in the local culture.

submitted a second annual health action plan to the local government. Many have specifically prioritized women's health issues, a promising outcome in a still patriarchal society.

During my time at Chirag, I had created inventory forms to inspect the standards of local government clinics. I discovered that health committees still used these forms as they steadily escalated their demands for accountability and access. Shanti Raikwal, a health committee member in Simayal, said, "Four months ago we visited the ANM centre (sub-center) and asked what supplies were available there. We just sent a petition to the PHC (Primary Health Center) that there should be a female doctor available."

Chirag's efforts in preventive health in the region are based on supporting existing institutions like health committees and motivating government health workers, such as ASHAs (Accredited Social Health Activists) and ANMs (Auxiliary Nursing Midwives). Madhavan said, "In the long run it makes sense to improve the government health system rather than run a parallel structure."

The progress I saw a year after I had left Chirag was both encouraging and enlightening. However, there were still barriers to effective community ownership over public health. The reach of health committees in villages was still limited due to the rugged, mountainous terrain. In some villages, health committees were barely functional. In other villages, despite Chirag's continued presence, only a few community members attended meetings. Even active health committees often remained dependent on Chirag staff in their operations.

On the last day of my return journey to Chirag, I wrote one last letter. The letter inquired about the delinquent status of a local government health clinic, due to open during my Fellowship year. I shared my observations and explained the benefits of a new, functioning health clinic. Writing a letter seemed a fitting exit, given the number of letters I had written during my Fellowship year. As a Fellow, I had spearheaded petition campaigns to resume missing supplies — Iron Folic Acid tablets for pregnant women and Vitamin A for children to prevent night blindness. Trekking from village to village, I requested *Gram Pradhans* to write letters of petition to the local government. After three months of follow-up visits and letters, which eventually reached the Chief Medical Officer, the missing supplies were resumed in the entire region.

While I was not sure what would come from my inquiry, I knew that what I could do remained in my hands. This letter, like my Fellowship year, was not simply about development or service. It was about home, my home. It was about who I am, and who I want to be.

With the perspective of time, enhanced by my recent visits to other Fellowship projects, I saw anew the challenges that I had struggled with a year before. In front of my eyes, my role as community organizer in rural India came back to life. I began to understand how each interaction mattered. Each meeting held, each letter sent, each health camp planned slowly added up to something much more powerful.

Looking back, one of the greatest lessons I have learned is to hold nothing back and trust the process. A part of this trust is the realization that just because you cannot see the change you are looking for does not mean it is not there. In a place where everything is so unfamiliar, why would change be so easily recognizable? Development, behavior change, and community empowerment can be slow processes. In both the larger picture of life and in rural development, long-term achievement is much more rewarding than immediate gratification.

As I pursue a Master of International Affairs degree, I carry my dog-eared journals, hand-scrawled bi-lingual notes, and countless interactions to the classroom. After graduation, I plan to return to the hills and apply my new knowledge. At Chirag, despite the commotion I caused, I have been told I always have a home there. My mother vehemently tells me that "enough is enough," and that I need to expand my horizons "internationally." Despite my plans to return, I do not know where life will take me. No matter what, I am sure that my education, experience, and heart will guide me to once more engage with people's movements. I attribute this to the constantly evolving perspective that I have gained through my personal experiments with social change.

"A small body of determined spirits, fired by an unquenchable faith in their mission can alter the course of history."

— *Mahatma Gandhi*

STAY ALIVE. STAY FIERCE.
by Dev Tayde

A few years back when I started carrying a cell phone, I gave up wearing a watch. The new phone technology redefines how I tell time. At Indicorps, we take it one step further. We encourage our people to redefine time itself. The length of a day is a function of the earth's latitude; the ability to stretch time is a function of living with purpose. The latter has been a constant driver for Team Indicorps.

The way we seek to stretch time does not require much. It simply requires greater self-awareness and infusion of purpose in everyday living. It asks us to look anew at what we do every moment: Is a train journey just a passage from point A to point B? Or is it a lesson in knowing India? Can you hear the incredible harmony of sounds in silence? What does chaos mute? Indicorps challenges each of us to embrace India, respect life, and lead with purpose. Indicorps keeps us on our toes all the time to create graceful service art; in that dance form, slipping from purposeful living is not an option.

Meet my team-mate Jaidip Patel. Jaidip completed three-and-a-half years of gruelling 50-hour shifts on oil-rigs in Gabon and Angola as penance for a return to India. Immediately after college in the summer of 2005, Jaidip interned at Indicorps as an Ultimate Frisbee coach for our sister project Ahmedabad Ultimate. Gifted with wings on his feet and an ability to connect to people, Jaidip overcame shyness and language barriers to connect with Indicorps and communities near the Gandhi Ashram. Smitten by the promise of India and Indicorps, Jaidip resolved to return to India upon completing his loan payments and larger family obligations. In 2008, Jaidip returned to India. He now leads operations for the Indicorps Fellowship program and for Ahmedabad Ultimate. Equally important to Jaidip's time in India is his role as big brother and role model for Janmesh and Meet — his host brothers, ages 9 and 6. Jaidip is a great example of the dedication and talent that helps shape Indicorps every year.

For me, Indicorps has played a role in only one-sixth of my life. Yet, that time frame has transformed the trajectory for the remainder. There have been ups and downs. Service has always been a part of my life; Indicorps has made it a way of life. A lot has happened during my Indicorps tenure. My grandmother — who was one of my greatest influences — passed away. I have dipped into the deepest reservoirs of patience and humility. As we enter a new decade of Indicorps Fellowships, I am confident that our processes hold infinite power. They are strong enough to pull people to lead a life that challenges them to incorporate purpose in their being; to earn their food, their sleep, their existence; and not to take anything for granted. Make "Earn your spot" a mantra for life.

You have read some undoubtedly profound stories about the impact of and on some amazing Indicorps Fellows. These stories are representative, but by no means, exhaustive. Whether staff, Fellows, interns, or short-term volunteers, Indicorps people interact with the world at a slightly different frequency and will continue to make an impact on the world. Indicorps people are central to launching a number of service-based programs in India (including the Youth Leadership Course, Young Professionals Initiative, Teach for India), India experience-based initiatives (Medic-India, InSpire, UK Learning Journeys, and IndiaGuide Gujarat), and a host of other amazing projects (LaborVoices, ThinkChange India, Seva Cafe, Global Rickshaw, etc).

While the landscape continues to change and people continue to redefine their interactions with India, we at Indicorps remain laser-focused in our approach to our communities and their needs, cutting out all the frills that distract from the purpose of serving. I consistently outpace the alarm no matter the previous day's activities. Exploring the vast expanse of possibilities with fellow projects, scanning prospective partner organizations, reaching out to prospective Fellows, or further sprucing Indicorps all promise a fulfilling day. The culmination of fulfilling days leads to a purposeful life.

I issue the same challenge to you as I do to each and every person who engages with Indicorps: Are you willing to wake up to the depths of your own purpose? What are you willing to do to find it? Are you blunt enough to face the mirror? We are a cutting-edge Fellowship. The cuts are deep; the edges sharp; the learning profound. We are excited to fully live each day. Are you?

Stay alive, stay fierce.

Dev Tayde

ACKNOWLEDGEMENTS

In India, at Indicorps, we are told there are no thank-yous between family, but this project would not have been possible without the guidance, support, and inspiration provided by so many. Sincere thanks are due to Sonal, Roopal, and Anand for their vision, the Indicorps family for their ever-present support, and the communities and organizations all over India that continue to create a better tomorrow.

I would like to especially thank: Anjali Desai and Rohan Jasani for guiding us when we were clueless, being patient with our endless questions, and doing a lot of everything — from editing to designing to counseling, Vijay Ramchandani for his artistic touch through his Worli drawings, design, and dedication in making this book a reality, Adam Ferguson for leading our charge and keeping us on track, and Dev Tayde for his wisdom and laughter when all that seemed real was utter frustration.

Chris Robert, Christina Mathews, Kohl Gill, and Rish Sanghvi for being editors, and being there — at all hours of day and night.

Pavi Krishnan for her poetry and vision of a world where every story matters.

I would like to express my gratitude to Senator Harris Wofford for his storied commitment to social justice and continued support to generations of youth who believe another world is possible.

I am humbled by, and grateful to, all those who continue to struggle for justice and work for peace on a daily basis, with the understanding that development is about living a life with dignity and service is about living a life of conviction.

The journey that allowed Journeys in Service was only possible because of: Rava *bhai* and Kora *behn*, Jayesh *bhai* and Anar *behn*,

Viren *bhai*, Ravi Gulati, Devdas Sripati, Mohar Ali, Sangeeta Zonbade, Prashant Dodke, Mansi Sanghvi, Shaheen Mistri, Arun and Tahirra Das, Sunil *bhau* and Nirupama *tai*, Rajendra Prasad Mugdul, Amrit Dhir, Karthik Raman, Kaushal Rajoriya, Dr. Ashok Agarwal, Amitava Banerjee, Devanand Srivastava, Prema Tiwari, VK Madhavan, Bhim Singh Negi, Pooja Shahani, Radha Shukla, Rakesh Pandey, Usha ji, Sowmya Somnath, Jared Buono, Dr. Seetharam, The Jani Family, The Mehta Family Foundation, Lakshmi Eassey, Tushar Kansal, Rahul Brahmbhatt, Nainesh *bhai* Joshi, Prerna Seth, Rashee Rohatgi, Terrell Levine, Jaidip Patel, Rohan Jasani, Alvir Sadhwani, Abhay Thakor, Roshini Kasad, Madhusudan Agarwal, Prithvi Ghorpade, Geetika Bhandari, Meera Madan, Vikram Madan, Lt. Gen HC Rai PVSM, Kanwal Rai, The Pahwa Family, my fellow Indicorps Alumni for their continued strength and inspiration, anyone who stopped by the Indicorps office for a few minutes, few hours, or few weeks and was asked to be a part of the process, and the countless strangers who fed me on trains when I was hungry, made room when I was sleeping on the floor, provided shelter from the rain, and were always willing to share their India.

A very special thank you to Roopal Shah for accepting nothing less than excellence, and always being a willing friend, critic, and mentor. Her leadership and heart of a champion kept this project going over time and space. *Journeys in Service* was only possible because of that spirit.

Gaurav Madan

February 2011
New York